KINGDOM

James T. Harman

**Prophecy
Countdown
Publications**

THE KINGDOM

Prophecy Countdown Publications
P.O. Box 941612
Maitland, FL 32794
www.ProphecyCountdown.com

Snowfall Press
1832 Woodmoor Drive, #211
Monument, Colorado 80132
www.Snowfallpress.com

ISBN: 978-0-9636984-1-4

All references from Scripture are from the King James Version unless noted otherwise. Words in bold emphasis are authors and not in original Scripture.

Scripture quotations from the Thompson Chain Reference Bible, New International Version (NIV), Copyright 1973, 1978 and 1984 by the International Bible Society.

Numerical references to selected words in the text of Scripture are from James H. Strong Dictionaries of the Hebrew and Greek words.

Certain words such as Kingdom and Judgement Seat are capitalized to emphasize their importance, but not in accordance with Traditional fashions.

The picture of the Milky Way on the front cover is credited to: E. L. Wrigh, (UCLA), The COBE Project, DIRBE, and NASA, Copyright © 2000.
The image on the back cover (M 81 82) is Copyright by Dietmar Hager
www.stargazer-observatory.com.

Prologue

The infrared picture of the Milky Way on the front cover can be found at the Astronomy Picture of the Day (APOD) website on 1/30/2000: http://antwrp.gsfc.nasa.gov/apod/ap000130.html.

It is important to understand that the Milky Way is only one of several hundred billions of galaxies in the Universe that God has created. Our Solar System is only one small part in the Milky Way, as depicted in the following artist's rendering:

http://chadlewis.net/tag/heaven/

The point is that our God is an awesome God who spoke this entire Universe into existence. The Universe is an immense creation that is too vast for the human mind to completely comprehend. And yet, God also created man to live on our tiny little planet called Earth. His plan for mankind is laid out in the Bible for everyone to read and follow.

This book has been written to touch on one segment of Biblical teaching called "The Kingdom." It is by no means a complete study of this important subject, however, there are very few modern authors who have correctly understood what God wants mankind to know. At the turn of the century, the Lord did raise up some godly men who did see the importance of "The Kingdom." Men such as: Robert Govett, D.M. Panton, G.H. Pember, G.H. Lang and Hudson Taylor were given much light and understanding of what is described as Kingdom truths.

Unfortunately, as the Church entered into the Laodicean age this century, most of their teachings have been disregarded, glossed over and forgotten. Fortunately, there still are a few writers who have taken the time to dig deep into God's Word to bring out this much-needed nourishment that is so badly lacking in the spiritual diet of most Christians.

Jesus spoke of the coming Kingdom many times. In His meeting with Nicodemus, Jesus said:

> *"Verily, verily, I say unto thee, Except a man be born again, he cannot **see** the kingdom of God."* (John 3:3)

In order to **see** the Kingdom of God, Jesus said man must be *"born again."* But now notice what Jesus said about **entering into** the Kingdom of God (the prerequisite for entrance):

> *"Jesus answered, Verily, verily, I say unto thee, Except a man be born of water and of the Spirit, he cannot **enter into** the kingdom of God."* (John 3:5)

Most Christians have been taught about the requirement of seeing the Kingdom of God. While being *"born again"* is the essential requirement, it is only part of our Lord's instructions. In the above verse, Jesus said we must be born of water and the Spirit in order to **enter into** the coming Kingdom of God.

This second part of our Lord's instruction on the Kingdom is what this book will address. While it will not be an exhaustive analysis of all facets of the Kingdom truths[1], it will hopefully whet the reader's appetite to dig into the Word of God for further study. The whole purpose of this book is to help Christians understand what seeking the Kingdom of God is all about, and thereby help them be among the chosen few who will be able to **enter into** the coming Kingdom.

Dedication

This book is dedicated to my wonderful wife Cindy, who originally taught me to be watching for the Lord to return. She has been an incredible soul mate who has weathered many trials and difficulties with me:

> *"Dear brothers, is your life full of difficulties and temptations? Then be happy, for when the way is rough, your patience has a chance to grow. So let it grow, and don't try to squirm out of your problems. For when your patience is finally in full bloom, then you will be ready for anything, strong in character, full and complete."* (James 1:2-4 – Living Bible)

Cindy has been a great friend and encourager, and hopefully together we will both be fortunate enough to each receive the rewards at the end of our journeys:

> *"Blessed is the man that endureth temptation: for when he is tried, he shall receive the crown of life, which the Lord hath promised to them that love him."*
> (James 1:12)

And I end this dedication by borrowing from the words of George N. H. Peter's dedication to his wife in his great work of: **_The Theocratic Kingdom_** (www.theocratickingdom.com):

> "…that our relationship here may qualify us the more
> for the fruition of each other's society in the predicted
> Theocracy of our Lord Jesus, the Christ, is the ardent
> prayer of your devoted
> Husband"

Acknowledgements

I want to acknowledge a few mature believers who have contributed greatly to my understanding of the Scripture.

I met Lyn Mize back in 1990, at Ray Brubaker's *International Prophecy Conference*. Lyn had just completed his book: *The Open Door*, and I had recently finished my book entitled: *The Coming Spiritual Earthquake*. We exchanged manuscripts at the time, and were both amazed how the Lord had given both of us similar messages for Christians living in the endtimes. Since then Lyn's studies and writings have far exceeded my own, and I have been truly blessed to call him my friend. His writings on the meat doctrines and deeper truths are extensive and can be found on his wonderful website: www.ffruits.org.

I am also indebted to Gary Whipple, who was the pastor of a local congregation that he led and of which I was fortunate to attend. Pastor Whipple has a great understanding of the deeper truths in Scripture and I have learned a great deal from his two great books: *Shock and Surprise Beyond the Rapture* and the *Matthew Mysteries*. While I am not in agreement with all of Pastor Whipple's conclusions, both are excellent studies for those interested in learning more about Kingdom truths.

Finally, I recently came into contact with Tom Finley, who has authored several fine books and articles that can be found on his website: www.seekersofchrist.org   His book, *Worthy of The Kingdom* is available on his site and it is a fantastic study that can help Christians be able to rule and reign with Christ in the coming Kingdom.

Table of Contents

Prologue iii
oreword   F 9
Preface 11

Chapter 1 – Grace and Works 13
Chapter 2 – The Judgement Seat of Christ 15
Chapter 3 – Salvation of the Soul 25
Chapter 4 – Seek First the Kingdom 29
Chapter 5 – Some Christians Miss the Kingdom 33
Chapter 6 – Outer Darkness 39
Chapter 7 – Hell - Sheol 45
                      Hades 45
                      Tartarus 46
                      Gehenna 47
Chapter 8 – The Second Death 53
Chapter 9 – The Book of Life 57
Chapter 10 – Overcomers 61
Chapter 11 – Enter the Kingdom 69

pilogue   E 79
Reference Notes 81

Appendix A – Watching for Jesus 87
Appendix B – Sign of Christ's Coming 89

Afterword 95

Special Invitation 99

What Readers Are Saying 102

WARNING ABOUT CONTENTS

If either Jesus or John the Baptist showed up today with a manuscript of their material, how many publishers do you think they would have to visit before they found one willing to carry their harsh messages?

> *"Woe to you, teachers of the law and Pharisees, you hypocrites! You shut the kingdom of heaven in men's faces. You yourselves do not enter, nor will you let those enter who are trying to."*
> (Matthew 23:13 – NIV)

> *"..Repent ye: for the kingdom of heaven is at hand. For this is he that was spoken of... one crying in the wilderness, Prepare ye the way of the Lord, make his paths straight."* (Matthew 3:2-3)

The many Christian publishing houses across our land would be hesitant to take on such a new title that would not be popularly received by the mainstream Church. Since they couldn't make a sufficient profit with their messages, they would probably have to send them on their way.

THE KINGDOM was written to help people realize that the Bible may have a difficult message that requires something of the believer. While you probably did not find this book in your local bookstore, be prepared to experience a paradigm shift in some of your Christian beliefs.

Foreword

Sir Isaac Newton, the great mathematician, scientist and Bible scholar made the following prediction about 300 years ago:

> "About the time of the end, a body of men will be raised up who will turn their attention to the prophecies, and insist upon their literal interpretation, in the midst of much clamour and opposition."
> Sir Isaac Newton (1643-1727 AD)

There is no doubt in my mind that Jim Harman is one of these men that God would raise up at the time of the end. Sir Isaac Newton also made another prediction that the End of the World (i.e., Age) would take place around 2012. Of course, it is not the world that will end but the Church Age, and it appears that Newton may be very close to being accurate on this prediction, as well. It is also important to understand that Sir Isaac Newton was against date setting about the time of the end, but he made this prediction nevertheless.

I met Jim at a prophecy conference in Tampa, Florida 19 years ago and we have been friends and fellow students of the Bible ever since that time. He and I agree on a great deal of Bible doctrine, and we are both looking forward to the Return of the Lord.

There is another prophecy about the time of the end that was addressed by Jesus Christ, and this prophecy is located in the Olivet Discourse. It is as follows:

> (Matt 24:45-47) *"Who then is a faithful and wise servant, whom his lord hath made ruler over his household, to give them meat in due season? Blessed is*

that servant, whom his lord when he cometh shall find so doing. Verily I say unto you, that he shall make him ruler over all his goods."

The information in this book certainly falls in the category of strong meat, and it is my firm conviction that Jim Harman will be one of these faithful and wise servants that provides "meat in due season".

Blaise Pascal, the famous French mathematician, physicist and religious philosopher made the following observation concerning Bible prophecies:

> "The prophecies are to be unintelligible to the ungodly but intelligible to those who are properly instructed." Blaise Pascal (1623 - 1662 AD)

I also firmly believe that Jim Harman is one of those Bible students who is properly instructed in the prophecies of the Bible, thus making him a godly man. Jim is a devout student of the Word of God, and he is open and teachable in the truths of Scripture. This is an absolute necessity for anyone to understand Bible prophecies, and Jim certainly lives up to this observation made by Blaise Pascal.

I recommend this book to anyone seeking the truths of Scripture. Jim is able to take the deeper truths of the Bible and explain them in simple language that can be understood by anyone who is open and teachable in Bible doctrine.

Lyn Mize, 08/29/09
Meat in Due Season Ministries
www.ffruits.org

Preface

As we approach the soon return of our Lord and Saviour Jesus Christ, everyone needs to be entirely sure they are really ready for what lies ahead.

Most Christians will tell you that they have accepted Jesus as their Saviour and that they are ready to meet Him. Sadly, most in the current Laodicean church age have no idea of what is about to transpire.

In Luke 18:8, Jesus asks:

> *"Nevertheless when the Son of man cometh, shall he find faith on the earth?"*

The churches are full of Christians who have accepted the Lord as their Saviour, but how many have the faith that Jesus is talking about?

One of the purposes of this book is to help Christians understand that coming to Christ (being "born again") is only the beginning of the faith relationship. If that faith is not properly cared for by a proper feeding from the Word, it will not mature into the faith that Jesus will be looking for.

Most pastors and teachers instruct their congregations in the *"milk"* doctrines of the faith while neglecting the vital *"meat"* doctrines that are so necessary for developing maturity in the faith:

> *"For every one that useth milk is unskilful in the word of righteousness: for he is a babe. But strong meat belongeth to them that are of full age, even those who by reason of use have their senses exercised to discern both good and evil".* (Hebrews 5:13-14)

This book contains a healthy diet of *"strong meat"* that will be hard for many Christians to digest. Because much of what follows goes against the "Traditions" that most have come to accept as truth, many will reject this study and continue in their captivity:

> *"See to it that no one takes you captive through hollow and deceptive philosophy, which depends on human tradition and the basic principles of this world rather than on Christ."* (Colossians 2:8 – NIV)

My prayer is that the reader will approach this study with an open mind and a teachable spirit and will have a true hunger to learn about the righteousness that Jesus will be looking for when He returns.

This book is written for the person who has been *"born again,"* as mentioned above, and as Jesus described to Nicodemus:

> *"Verily, verily, I say unto thee, Except a man be born again, he cannot see the kingdom of God."* (John 3:3)

If you have not been born again, then you need to believe on the Lord Jesus Christ for salvation today. Paul put it simply:

> *"..if you confess with your mouth, 'Jesus is Lord,' and believe in your heart God raised him from the dead, you will be saved."* (Romans 10:9 – NIV)
> *"...everyone who calls on the name of the Lord will be saved."* (Romans 10:13 – NIV)

Some have called it "easy believism," but the salvation that Jesus offers is free. Call upon Him now and He will save you. Also, please see the ***Special Invitation*** at the end of this book.

Get out your Bible and get ready for a delicious meal of *"meat."* You are about to feast upon the wonderful truths of Christ's and the Apostle's teachings that can save your soul (your spirit was saved when you believed in Christ) and help you gain your entrance into the coming Kingdom and to rule and reign with Him over the beautiful Universe that He created!

Chapter 1 – Grace and Works

Among Christians today, one of the greatest reasons for the lack of proper understanding about grace is due to the failure in distinguishing between the doctrines of grace and works. Most believers can probably quote Ephesians 2:8-9:

> "*For by grace are ye saved through faith; and that not of yourselves: it is the gift of God: Not of works, lest any man should boast.*" (Ephesians 2:8-9)

These verses describe the fundamental doctrine that our salvation is a free gift from God and that man's works do not have anything to do with our salvation. The doctrine of grace is a vital part of our Christian faith.

The problem begins when most Christians completely disregard the verse that follows:

> "*For we are his workmanship, created in Christ Jesus unto **good works**, which God hath before ordained that we should walk in them.*" (Ephesians 2:10)

> "*For we are God's workmanship, created in Christ Jesus to **do good works**, which **God prepared in advance for us to do.***" (Ephesians 2:10 – NIV)

It is important to reiterate that works are not required of anyone to be saved. Salvation is a 100% free gift. Man can do nothing to earn it and there is nothing that we can do to lose it. Salvation is completely received as a gift from God by faith in Christ.

While works are not required for our salvation, the above verse indicates that once a person is saved, God has prepared good works that He wants us to do. Why does He want us to do good works? Because He wants to give His children rewards:

> *"And, behold, I come quickly; and my* **reward** *is with me, to give every man according as his* **work** *shall be."* (Revelation 22:12)

When Jesus Christ returns, He is coming to reward His faithful followers for the good works that they have performed for Him!

Unfortunately, most Christians believe they will automatically receive rewards due to the fact they have been saved. They have not been properly taught that which the Word of God actually says:

> *Salvation is by grace, but rewards are given according to works!*

The misunderstanding over the doctrine of grace and the doctrine of rewards has robbed the Church of the many prizes which God wants to give.   In the next chapter we will review the five major Crowns that Christians can earn at the Judgement Seat of Christ.

As we continue in this study, it is imperative to remember that works are not required to be saved. Salvation is completely by faith in Jesus Christ.   Once a person is saved, then works become a vital ingredient in their future. God has ordained the good works that He wants every believer to do. If we fail in accomplishing the mission He has for us, we may be very disappointed when we arrive at the Judgement Seat of Christ.

Chapter 2 – The Judgement Seat of Christ

All believers should be aware of what will take place very soon:

> *"For **we must all appear before the judgement seat of Christ**; that every one may receive the things done in his body, according to that he hath done, whether it be good or bad."* (II Corinthians 5:10)

As we approach the time of the Lord's return, it is vital that everyone understands what lies ahead after we are taken to be with the Lord. Notice that the above Scripture says that we will all appear before the Judgement Seat of Christ. This is a <u>Judgement Seat</u> before our Lord, to give an account for our lives and all that we have done, whether good or bad.

SHOCK AND SURPRISE

While we long to be with our precious Lord and Saviour, we wonder how many are really ready to face the Judgement Seat of Christ? We even ask ourselves, are we ready to meet Jesus?

After the Rapture takes place, many Christians will experience a great deal of shock and surprise.[2] The Lukewarm believers will be left on the earth to face their time of testing under the Antichrist; while the faithful, wise believers will be taken to be with the Lord forever! (See Luke 21:36, Rev. 7:14, Rev. 3:10).

What is it that distinguishes between these two groups? Why were some wise and why were some foolish? Why were some ready, while others were taken by surprise like a thief?

As mentioned in the previous chapter, most church leaders have not taught us properly regarding grace and works: *Salvation is by grace, but rewards are given according to works!*

The Judgement Seat of Christ will be the time when the

faithful Christians will be rewarded for their faithfulness in doing the good works God ordained for them to do. Likewise, for the unfaithful and foolish Christians, the Judgement Seat will be a time of great disappointment:

> *"Knowing therefore the terror of the Lord, we persuade men..."* (II Corinthians 5:11)

The Church loves to hear sermons on the love of God, but few pastors and teachers are brave enough to talk about the *"terror of the Lord."* The Judgement Seat of Christ will not be a pleasant experience for those Christians who have been living unfaithful lives. All deeds, true motives and designs will be laid bare before the Lord. The Christian "Ministry" of many believers will be revealed as a means to further their own personal aspirations of wealth and fame rather than bringing glory to the Lord.

Now is the time that all Christians should be living their lives in view of the Judgement Seat of Christ and the rewards (Crowns) that can be earned for their faithful lives. Jesus warned us ahead of time that many will try to take these crowns from the believers:

> *"Behold, I come quickly: hold that fast which thou hast, that no man take thy crown."* (Revelation 3:11)

Jesus was telling his Church to hold on to that *"which thou hast"* so that it would not lose their Crowns. The Word of God shows there are five different Crowns that are possible for Christians to earn. All Christians should be earnestly striving for these rewards so that they may cast them unto Jesus in the very near future:

> *"The four and twenty elders fall down before him that sat on the throne and worship him that liveth forever and ever, and **cast their crowns before the throne**, saying, "Thou art worthy, O Lord, to receive glory*

and honor and power: for thou hast created all things, and for thy pleasure they are and were created."

(Revelation 4:10-11)

What a glorious day that will be when we are able to worship our great God! Will you have crowns to lay at His feet? Let's see what the five possible crowns are and how they can be obtained.

CROWN
OF
LIFE   .

> *"Blessed is the man that endureth temptation: for when he is tried, he shall receive the **crown of life**, which the Lord hath promised to them that love him."* (James 1:12)

The Crown of Life is the first and basic crown. It is given to those Christians who truly love Jesus. Because they love Him, they are faithful to Him. When trials and tests arrive in their lives, they remain true to Him. They are overcomers who endure temptations and win this crown for remaining faithful to Jesus.

INCORRUPTIBLE
CROWN

> *"Know ye not that they which run in a race run all, but one receiveth the prize? So run, that ye may obtain. And every man that striveth for the mastery is temperate in all things. Now they do it to obtain a corruptible crown; but we an **incorruptible**. I therefore so run... But I keep my body and bring it into subjection...lest I be a castaway."* (I Corinthians 9:24-25)

The Incorruptible Crown is awarded to the Christian who wins the spiritual race that is set before each believer. It is a daily race in which the sins of the flesh must be put off by allowing the Holy Spirit to take control. It is not won until the race is over, and even the Apostle Paul was concerned that he might not win this prize. Yes, even Paul was concerned that he might be a castaway. This should be a lesson for everyone who says it doesn't matter how you live after you are saved. Even the great Apostle Paul was concerned for his own life.

To win this crown, the believer must be successful in *"crucifying the flesh,"* as is described in Galatians 5:16, 19-26, and by turning from the things of this world.

CROWN
OF
RIGHTEOUSNESS

> *"I have fought a good fight, I have finished my course, I have kept the faith: Henceforth there is laid up for me a* **crown of righteousness**, *which the Lord, the righteous judge, shall give me at that day: and not to me only, but unto all them also that love his appearing."*
> (II Timothy 4:7-8)

The Crown of Righteousness is the next level of reward. It is given for keeping the true faith, i.e., keeping God's Word. Directly associated with keeping the faith is *"loving his appearing."* Living in the endtime, you would think that all Christians would receive this crown. And yet, very few modern day Christians even care to discuss the return of the Lord. Paul is saying that those Christians who are alert, and anxiously looking for the Lord to return, are the ones who are keeping the faith. Those who long for that great day are given the wonderful promise of receiving the Crown of Righteousness.

CROWN
OF
REJOICING

> *"For what is our hope, or joy, or **crown of rejoicing**?*
> *Are not even ye in the presence of our Lord Jesus Christ*
> *at his coming? For ye are our glory and joy."*
>
> (I Thessalonians 2:19-20)

The last two crowns may be the highest rewards of the five crowns. The Crown of Rejoicing is also known as the soul winner's crown.

In the above verse, Paul was referring to the very faithful Christians from Thessalonica. Paul was instrumental in helping them become faithful Christians who were counted worthy of entering the Kingdom. Because of this, they are seen as holy evidence before Jesus Christ at His return. Their faithfulness to this high calling provided their entrance into the Kingdom, and as a result, Paul saw their faithful lives as a Crown of Rejoicing when the Lord returns.

Likewise, those Christians who teach others and lead others into a deeper relationship with Jesus will also receive the Crown of Rejoicing when the Lord comes. While winning people into a saving knowledge of Christ is important, this crown is given to those who are actually helping other Christians to become faithful disciples, and thereby helping them to gain their own entrance into the coming Kingdom.

Solomon put it this way:

> *"...he who wins souls is wise."*
> (Proverbs 11:30 – NKJV)

CROWN
OF
GLORY

> *"Be shepherds of God's flock that is under your care,*
> *serving as overseers, not because you must, but because*
> *you are willing, as God wants you to be; not greedy for*
> *money but eager to serve; not lording it over those*
> *entrusted to you, but being examples to the flock. And*
> *when the Chief Shepherd appears, you will receive the*
> ***crown of glory*** *that will never fade away."* (I Pet.5:2-4)

The Crown of Glory is given to the faithful under-shepherd who properly feeds the sheep. This is any Christian who has matured in the faith and who is teaching others the true teachings from the Word of God. When Jesus comes, they will receive the Crown of Glory. Let's briefly review the five possible Crowns and how they are earned:

THE 5 CROWNS

CROWN OF LIFE
Be faithful, be baptized and patiently endure the present trials and testings in life. Die to self.

INCORRUPTIBLE CROWN
Be filled with the Spirit. Put off fleshly desires.

CROWN OF RIGHTEOUSNESS
Mature in the Word. Keep the faith. Love His appearing.

CROWN OF REJOICING
Be a soul winner. Lead other Christians into a deeper relationship with Jesus, helping them gain the Kingdom.

CROWN OF GLORY
Learn the Scriptures. Nourish the flock of God with the deeper truths from God's Word.

As mentioned earlier, Jesus warned us not to let any man take our crowns. Let's look at each crown, and see how others can make us lose our crowns.

Crown of Life

The Crown of Life is given to those who patiently endure the present trials and tests that come in this life. Those who are overcomers will receive this crown as a reward for their faithfulness. Others can take this crown from the believer through false teaching. Most of the Church has not been taught what it really means to be an overcomer. By so doing, most Christians will not gain this most basic crown.

Most believers feel that they are automatically overcomers by virtue of their salvation. They have never allowed the Holy Spirit to teach them how to really experience His overcoming power in their life. Sadly, false teaching has robbed most of the Church of this most basic reward.

Incorruptible Crown

The incorruptible crown is given to those faithful believers who allow the Spirit to be the master over their flesh. Others will try to take this crown from you by telling you that it doesn't matter how you live after you are saved. They will say, "Go sow a few wild oats," or "You are saved by Grace, don't worry about it."

The worldly Laodicea church age is filled with Christians who have given in to the desires of the flesh. Don't listen to them; don't let them take your crown. The small pleasures this world has to offer pale in comparison to the many astounding things God has awaiting His faithful.

Crown of Righteousness

This crown is given to those who keep the faith, and love His appearing. Others will try to take this crown from you by trying to get you to give up looking for the Lord's return. This can happen in two ways. Most in the Church are not interested in speaking about the Rapture. By so doing, these believers can discourage your faith and hope in the Lord's coming; thereby causing you to lose your crown. The second way is through the many false alarms that have sounded. Don't cease looking for Jesus! He said He is coming again, and He will return at just the right moment, and not one day late! Don't let others take this crown from you.

Crown of Rejoicing

The soul winner's crown is given to those who are actually leading other Christians into a deeper relationship with Jesus. This crown has been stolen from most in the Church today because the doctrine of rewards is not understood or taught. Don't let this keep you from earning this reward. Help others to be faithful disciples of Christ.

Crown of Glory

The Crown of Glory is given to those who are found nourishing God's flock. Others will try to take this crown from you by telling you that it is reserved for the Pastor. Sadly, many Pastors are not properly feeding the flock of God today. This crown is God's reward to those who know and love God's Word sufficiently to teach others the real truth. Be faithful to Him, and He will give you this reward very, very soon!

All Christians should be actively seeking all of the above crowns. These crowns are rewards for faithfully serving the Lord. God has ordained the *"good works"* He wants every believer to perform, and those who are faithful will be richly rewarded for their humble accomplishments in His service.

However, many Christians will arrive at the Judgement Seat of Christ without even one crown. These Christians will be saved, but they will not receive any rewards due to their unfruitful and unfaithful lives.

While these Christians are saved, their lack of rewards are an indictment of their failure to abide in Christ for His direction in their lives:

> *"And now, little children, **abide in him**; that, when he shall appear, we may have confidence, and **not be ashamed** before him at his coming."* (I John 2:28)

Regrettably, many Christians will be ashamed when Jesus returns because they failed in the missions that God had ordained for their lives. While their spirit was saved, they failed to work out their salvation and thereby secure the salvation of their soul.

> *"Wherefore, my beloved, as ye have always obeyed, not as in my presence only, but now much more in my absence, **work out your own salvation** with fear and trembling."* (Philippians 2:12)

In the next chapter, we will look further into what it means to save your soul and to work out your salvation.

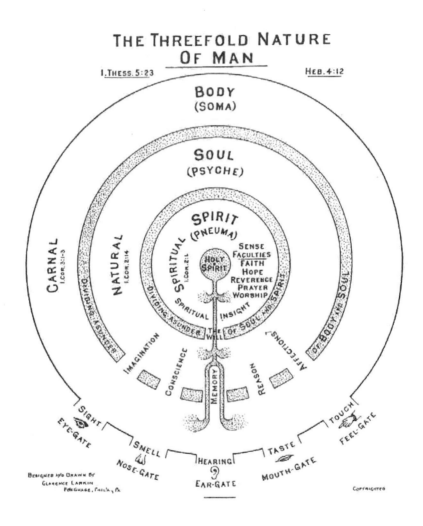

The above diagram is from ***Dispensational Truth***, by Clarence Larkin, page 99, © 1918.   Used with permission of the Rev. Clarence Larkin Estate, P.O. Box 334, Glenside, PA   19038, U.S.A., 215-576-5590, *www.larkinestate.com*

Chapter 3 – Salvation of the Soul

SPIRIT, SOUL AND BODY

Man's nature is made up with three parts: spirit, soul and body. This truth is brought out by Paul in I Thessalonians 5:23:

> "...and I pray God your whole spirit and soul and body be preserved blameless unto the coming of our Lord Jesus Christ."

Paul prayed for each of the three parts of man. Each is distinct and each has its own destiny.

SPIRIT

Once a person is born again, the Holy Spirit takes up residence in the believer (pictured in the diagram on the preceding page). The Holy Spirit comes and resides in every person who has been saved. The person's spirit is saved and guaranteed to be with God for eternity. As outlined in Chapter 1, the salvation of a person's spirit is completely free and cannot be earned:

> "For by grace are ye saved through faith; and that not of yourselves: it is the gift of God: Not of works, lest any man should boast." (Ephesians 2:8-9)

The **salvation of the spirit** is 100% free. There is nothing anyone can do in order to earn it, and nothing anyone can do in order to lose it. Once a person is saved, his spirit can never be lost again because it is saved by the gracious gift of God. That person's spirit is guaranteed to be with God for eternity.

SOUL

After a person's spirit is saved, a battle begins for that person's soul. God wants to see the soul saved, but Satan and the person's flesh will try to see it destroyed. The Holy Spirit wants to save the person's soul, and the whole goal of one's faith should be the **salvation of the soul**:

> *"Receiving the end of your faith, even the salvation of your souls."* (I Peter 1:9)

Unfortunately, this teaching has been all but lost in the current modern day Church. Christ's teaching on the salvation of the soul and the coming Millennial Kingdom have been disregarded by the lukewarm 20th century body of Christ. False doctrines, materialism and other forms of idols have taken pre-eminence in the average believer's life.

Our Lord's words found in Matthew 16:26 are quite pertinent for today:

> *"For what is a man profited, if he shall gain the whole world, and **lose his own soul**?"*

The context of this verse is to believers because He was speaking to His disciples. Jesus is telling us that it is possible for believers to lose their own soul.

The body of the carnal man is in a war with the spirit man for the soul. The spirit wants to save the soul, but the body wants to gratify itself. If the flesh wins the battle, then the soul is lost!

The answer to the war that is going on within every true believer was given to us by Jesus:

> *"...If any man will come after me, let him deny himself, and take up his cross, and follow me. For whosoever will save his life shall lose it: and whosoever will lose his life for my sake shall find it."* (Matthew 16:24-25)

In order for the soul to be saved, the believer is required to deny himself and lose his own life for Christ's sake. In other words, the person who wants to save his soul must be willing to die to himself and take up the cross Christ gives him to bear. If the believer is unwilling to give up his own life for Christ's sake, he will treasure worldly riches and pleasures in exchange for his own soul.

Remember, the **salvation of the spirit** is 100% free and impossible to earn by works. In the above teaching, however, Jesus is instructing the believer on how to **save the soul**.

To save the soul, the believer has to perform certain works: deny self, take up his cross and then follow Jesus. This could not be the salvation of the spirit because works are involved. Jesus was teaching the salvation of the soul, and he wants to make sure that the believer does save his soul.

NOT WORTHY OF ME

The Lord brought out the salvation of the soul in another way:

> *"He that loveth father or mother more than me is not worthy of me; and he that loveth son or daughter more than me is not worthy of me. And he that taketh not his cross and followeth after me, is not worthy of me. He that findeth his life shall lose it; and he that loseth his life for my sake shall find it."* (Matthew 10:38-39)

Here again, Jesus is teaching on the salvation of the soul. He calls it "being worthy of Him," and it requires something of the believer. This could not be the salvation of the spirit, since works are involved. In view here then, is the salvation of the soul. In order to save the soul and to be considered worthy, the believer must give up his right to everything and to everybody. Yes, even close relatives must not come before one's love and devotion to Jesus.

In order to save one's soul, the believer's life must be lost for His sake. For the soul to be saved, the desires of the flesh (body) must be given up to the desires of the Spirit. Taking up one's cross is to crucify the desires of the flesh and to allow the Spirit to control the believer's life. By forsaking one's life for Christ's sake, the believer allows the Spirit to rule; thus saving the soul.

CARNAL VS. SPIRITUAL

This teaching on the salvation of the soul is critical to the well being of the believer. If the flesh (body) is allowed to control the **life** of the believer, their soul will be lost. The carnal believer allows the flesh to rule over the spirit. While the carnal Christian has a saved spirit, their soul is in danger of perishing.

The carnal believer wants to keep their worldly pleasures and viewpoints of power, wealth and success in order to gratify self. By keeping or saving this life, they will end up losing their soul.

The carnal believer is pictured in the Old Testament story of Esau who for one morsel of food sold his birthright (Hebrews 12:16-17). The carnal Christian is more concerned with the here and now than with the future Kingdom. By being as shortsighted as Esau, the carnal Christian will be very disappointed if they don't put Christ first in their life before it is too late.

The spiritual believer, on the other hand, is concerned with the salvation of their own soul. The spiritual believer gives up all claims to worldly interests and is more interested in following Jesus. They allow their spirit to overcome the flesh through the Holy Spirit's help; thereby saving their own soul.

The salvation of the soul is the goal of one's faith, and it should be the priority of every born-again believer. Directly related to the salvation of the soul is entrance into the coming Kingdom that will commence once Jesus returns. Entrance into the coming Kingdom is directly linked to the salvation of the soul. The believer who successfully saves his soul at the Judgement Seat of Christ assures his entrance into the Kingdom.

Chapter 4 – Seek First the Kingdom

The Kingdom is the 1,000 year Millennium when Jesus will rule and reign the earth. The Kingdom is rapidly approaching and the vast majority of the Church is completely unaware of the ramifications. Let's look at an important text which is highly misunderstood:

> "...seek ye first the kingdom of God, and his righteousness: and all these things shall be added unto you." (Matthew 6:33)

Notice Jesus says, "seek ye first the kingdom of God, and his righteousness." Many leave this part of the verse out in their interpretations. So many have used this verse to motivate other Christians to either give to their organization, or to require them to get active in their "Christian" program. This is not the purpose that Jesus spoke these words.

ENTRANCE INTO THE KINGDOM

Jesus is telling the Christian that the number one priority should be seeking His Kingdom and His righteousness. To seek this means to seek entrance into the coming Kingdom. The first priority for every Christian should be their own entrance into the Kingdom!

Sadly, the majority of Christians are too preoccupied with man's agenda on this present earthly Kingdom to be concerned with the coming Millennial Kingdom. While they pray the words, "Thy kingdom come..." how many understand what they are praying, and how many really mean it and really want the Kingdom of God to come?

The reason for this misunderstanding, and the current lukewarmness that pervades the modern Church, lies with the false teachings fostered by our spiritual leaders! Just as in the time of Christ, modern day teachers are leading the people off the correct path:

> *"Woe to you, teachers of the law and Pharisees, you hypocrites! You shut the kingdom of heaven in men's faces. You yourselves do not enter, nor will you let those enter who are trying to."* (Matthew 23:13 – NIV)

Today's spiritual leaders are doing the exact same thing that the Pharisees did at the time Jesus spoke these words. They are not entering into the coming Kingdom, and they are also keeping the vast majority of believers from entering. If Jesus were here today, He would say to many of the prophecy teachers and leaders: Hypocrites! It is time to deny self and follow me before it is too late!

SEEK RIGHTEOUSNESS

As will be discussed in the chapter that follows, some Christians will miss the Kingdom of God when Jesus comes to reign upon the earth. Let's look at what is required in order to gain our entrance. In Matthew 6:33, Jesus says to seek first the Kingdom and his righteousness. Now notice what Jesus said earlier in His Sermon on the Mount:

> *"For I say unto you, That except your righteousness shall exceed the righteousness of the scribes and Pharisees, ye shall in no case enter into the kingdom of heaven."* (Matthew 5:20)

Yes, Jesus is telling the Christian that their righteousness must exceed the righteousness of even the spiritual leaders of the day. We need to remember that the Christian's righteousness is based upon the imputed righteousness of Christ that is obtained by faith:

> *"Even the righteousness of God which is by faith of*
> *Jesus Christ unto all and upon all them that believe..."*
> (Romans 3:22)

Faith in Jesus Christ is the only thing that will justify a person before God. The believer receives the righteousness of God by faith in Jesus Christ + nothing.

Remember that we learned earlier that the whole goal of our faith is the salvation of our soul. After a person receives the righteousness of God through faith in Jesus Christ, they must also "hunger and thirst after righteousness" if they are to be filled with God's Spirit. Only after the believer receives God's righteousness can they live righteously as God requires:

> *"That the righteousness of the law might be fulfilled in*
> *us, who walk not after the flesh, but after the Spirit. For*
> *they that are after the flesh do mind the things of the*
> *flesh; but they that are after the Spirit the things of the*
> *Spirit."* (Romans 8:4-5)

While the Christian is justified through faith in the sight of God, the believer is **required to continue to walk after the Spirit** and not after the flesh. The believer must earnestly seek God's righteousness by being led by the Spirit of God and not by the flesh. Only in this way will the Christian's righteousness exceed that of the scribes and Pharisees, and thereby gain them entrance into the Kingdom of heaven.

This truth is also seen in the description of the Bride of Christ:

> *"Let us rejoice and be glad and give him glory! For the*
> *wedding of the Lamb has come, and **His bride has made***
> ***herself ready**. Fine linen, bright and clean, was given*

> *her to wear. Fine linen stands for the **righteous acts** of the saints."* (Revelation 19:6-8 – NIV)

The righteous acts or deeds of the saints are the things that set the Bride of Christ apart. She made herself ready for the wedding by obtaining her fine linen, which represents her righteous works after she was saved. The original Greek confirms that this wedding garment is not the righteousness that is imputed to every believer, but represents the **righteous acts** or **righteous living** of the believer. The Bride of Christ longs to be with her Bridegroom and she is actively seeking His righteousness and His Kingdom in her daily walk.

Entrance into the coming Kingdom will only be obtained by those who are truly seeking that entrance during the present time, and by those who are truly seeking His righteousness. As we will see in the following chapter, some Christians will indeed not gain entrance into the Kingdom.

Chapter 5 - Some Christians Miss the Kingdom

As discussed previously, the Kingdom refers to the 1,000-year reign with Christ known as the Millennium. Not all born-again believers are assured of taking part in this Kingdom:

> *"Not everyone who says to me, 'Lord, Lord,' will enter the kingdom of heaven, but only he who does the will of my Father who is in heaven."* (Matthew 7:21 – NIV)

The above Scripture is near the very end of the Sermon on the Mount. In this great sermon, the Lord taught us many wonderful things about entrance into the Kingdom.

First of all, please notice that Jesus is talking about Christians. They are saying to Him, *"Lord, Lord..."* I Corinthians tells us:

> *"Therefore I tell you that no one is speaking by the Spirit of God says, "Jesus be cursed" and no one can say, "Jesus is Lord," except by the Holy Spirit."*
> (I Corinthians 12:3 – NIV)

The above teaches that only through the Holy Spirit can a person call Jesus their Lord. This is proof that the individuals Jesus was referring to at the end of his sermon were indeed Christians. They were calling Jesus Lord.

Not only did they call Him Lord, which tells us they were legitimate believers; they also performed many wonderful works:

> *"Many will say to me on that day, Lord, Lord, did we not prophesy in your name, and in your name drive out demons and perform many miracles?"*
> (Matthew 7:22 – NIV)

From this we can see that these were active believers in Christ who did perform many good works. They prophesied in His name, cast out demons and performed many miracles. They were true believers who had been born again. They were even doing many great and wonderful works, but, notice what the Lord says to them:

> *"...I never knew you; depart from Me, you who practice lawlessness!"*
> (Matthew 7:23)

The word for *"knew"* (#1097) in the above verse can best be translated as: to be intimately acquainted with. In other words, although these born-again individuals did many great works for Jesus, He never really knew them the way that He desired. While they knew Him as their Saviour, they had not really gotten acquainted with Him in an intimate way, in order to make Him the <u>true</u> <u>Lord</u> OVER <u>their</u> <u>soul</u>.

As a result, these Christians were turned away by the Lord. Does this mean that they lost their salvation?

No, not at all. Salvation is 100% free and it can <u>never</u> be taken away. There is nothing anyone can do in order to earn their salvation, and there is nothing they can do to lose it. Salvation is completely free and secure.

These Christians did not lose their salvation, but they were turned away by the Lord, and they did not gain entrance into the Kingdom. This is the 1,000-year reign with Christ that begins after the Lord returns.

These believers will not enter into the Kingdom and rule and reign with Christ because they failed to know Him properly, and they failed to give up their present life for Christ. Their

Christian endeavor had apparently been motivated by the flesh and was not a result of the Holy Spirit's direction and control.

This is a sober warning to the Christian. We all need to examine the motives of our hearts. Are our Christian works meant to glorify God, or to glorify self? If we are really active in our Christian endeavors for ourselves, Christ will tell us, *"away from me, I never knew you."*

These are our Lord's own words: that not all Christians will enter the Kingdom, or the 1,000-year reign with Him. In addition to the above, the Lord taught that only the worthy would be in the Kingdom:

> *"But those who are considered WORTHY of taking part in THAT AGE and in the resurrection from the dead..."*
> (Luke 20:35 – NIV)

Jesus said only those who are considered WORTHY will take part in THAT AGE or the Kingdom age, which begins at the first resurrection (see Chapter 10 for more on this subject).

LIVE BY THE SPIRIT

In addition to the teachings by our Lord about Christians missing the Kingdom, the Apostle Paul gives us many more examples, which should have an equally sobering effect for those Christians who are not truly being led by the Spirit of God. The few examples given below require no commentary:

> *"So I say, live by the Spirit, and you will not gratify the desires of the sinful nature ...The acts of the sinful nature are obvious: sexual immorality, impurity and debauchery; idolatry and witchcraft; hatred, discord, jealousy, fits of rage, selfish ambition, dissensions, factions and envy; drunkenness, orgies, and the like. I*

warn you, as I did before, that those who live like this <u>*will not inherit the kingdom of God.*</u> *"*
(Galatians 5:16, 19-21 – NIV)

"But among you there must not be even a hint of sexual immorality, or of any kind of impurity, or of greed, because these are improper for God's holy people. Nor should there be obscenity, foolish talk or coarse joking, which are out of place, but rather thanksgiving. For of this you can be sure: No immoral, impure or greedy person – such a man is an idolater – has <u>*any inheritance in the kingdom of Christ and of God.*</u> *Let no one deceive you with empty words, for because of such things God's wrath comes on those who are disobedient."*
(Ephesians 5:3-6 – NIV)

"Since, then, you have been raised with Christ, set your hearts on things above, where Christ is seated at the right hand of God. Set your minds on things above, not on earthly things. For you died, and your life is now hidden with Christ in God. When Christ, who is your life, appears, then you also will appear with him in glory. Put to death, therefore, whatever belongs to your earthly nature: sexual immorality, impurity, lust, evil desires and greed, which is idolatry. <u>*Because of these, the wrath of God is coming.*</u> *You used to walk in these ways, in the life you once lived. But now* <u>*you must rid yourselves of all such things as these:*</u> *anger, rage, malice, slander, and filthy language from your lips. Do not lie to each other, since you have taken off your old self with its practices and have put on the new self, which is being renewed in knowledge in the image of its Creator."*
(Colossians 3:1-10 – NIV)

For final evidence that not all Christians will be in the coming Kingdom, notice how Paul prayed for the disciples in Thessalonica:

> *"Which is a manifest token of the righteous judgement of God, that ye **may be counted worthy** of the **kingdom of God**, for which ye also suffer."* (II Thessalonians 1:5)

> *"Wherefore also we **pray always** for you, that our God would **count you worthy of this calling**..."*
> (II Thessalonians 1:11)

Paul knew that the disciples in Thessalonica were exemplary Christians (see I Thessalonians 1 & II Thessalonians 1:1-4). And yet Paul constantly prayed that they may be counted worthy of the high calling of entering into the Kingdom of God. If all Christians automatically enter the Kingdom, then Paul's concern and prayer would have been completely unnecessary.

Courtesy of: www.capemaywedding.net
(Credit to: Michael Leslie)

Chapter 6 - Outer Darkness

We have seen that all Christians will appear before the Judgement Seat of Christ to give an account of their life. Those who have lived a faithful and obedient life will receive rewards. They have been successful in saving their soul and will be granted entrance into the coming Kingdom.

Those Christians who are unfaithful and disobedient will **not** enter into the Kingdom. They arrive at the Judgement Seat of Christ and fail to receive any rewards since they were unsuccessful in saving their soul in this life. Sadly, as a result of their unfruitful life, they will be turned away by the Lord and will not granted entrance into the coming Kingdom.

KINGDOM = 1,000 YEARS

It is important to remember that the Millennial reign with Christ in the coming Kingdom will last for 1,000 years.

> *"...and they lived and reigned with Christ a thousand years."* (Revelation 20:4)

Unfortunately, some Christians will **not** enter into this thousand year reign with Christ. While they will miss going into the Kingdom, this does not mean that they will go to hell as some believe. Remember, everyone who has been *"born again"* goes to heaven and will see the Kingdom:

> *"Verily, verily, I say unto thee, Except a man be born again, he cannot **see** the kingdom of God."* (John 3:3)

All those who are Christians will either see the Kingdom or enter into the Kingdom. All Christians will be with God in eternity, but unfaithful and disobedient Christians will miss the opportunity of ruling and reigning with Christ for 1,000 years.

We will now look at what happens to those Christians who fail to enter into the coming Kingdom. It is important to point out that not everyone is in agreement about all of the details as to where the coming Kingdom will be. Some teach it will be on the earth while others believe it will be from the new Jerusalem in heaven. The purpose of this brief study is not to analyze all of the details and answer all of these questions. The purpose of this review is to show that participation in the coming Kingdom is something that is ether gained ("entered into") or lost ("not entered") by the Christian, and what failure to be part of the 1,000-year reign means.

OUTER DARKNESS – JEWS

Outer darkness is a phrase that is only mentioned three times in the New Testament. Jesus used this phrase in addressing three different classes of people. The first time He used the term was in regard to the Jews:

> *"And I say unto you, That many shall come from the east and west, and shall sit down with Abraham, and Isaac, and Jacob, in the kingdom of heaven. But the children of the kingdom shall be cast out into **outer darkness**: there shall be weeping and gnashing of teeth."*
> (Matthew 8:11-12)

The context of the above verse relates to the Jews. Here Jesus points out that some will be able to sit down with Abraham, Isaac and Jacob in the coming Kingdom. However, He also points out that some will be cast out into outer darkness. This separation among the Jews is similar to that described for the two other groups.

OUTER DARKNESS – GENTILES

The next time Jesus used the phrase *"outer darkness"* was in the parable of the Gentiles during the Tribulation period found in Matthew 22: 1-14.

> *"And when the king came in to see the guests, he saw there a man which had not on a wedding garment: And he saith unto him, Friend, how camest thou in hither not having a wedding garment? And he was speechless. Then said the king to the servants, Bind him hand and foot, and take him away, and cast him into **outer darkness**; there shall be weeping and gnashing of teeth. For many are called, but few are chosen."*
> (Matthew 22:11-14)

In this parable, Jesus shows that some of the Gentiles who are saved during the Tribulation period will arrive at the wedding feast without a *"wedding garment."* This garment is similar to the fine linen worn by the Bride of Christ:

> *"Let us rejoice and be glad and give him glory! For the wedding of the Lamb has come, and his bride has made herself ready.* ***Fine linen****, bright and clean, was given her to wear (Fine linen stands for the **righteous acts of the saints.)* "* (Revelation 19:7-8 – NIV)

The Bride of Christ arrives at her wedding wearing the fine linen wedding garment, which is a result of her righteous acts, or righteous living after she was saved (see Strong's #1345: a righteous act or deed). In contrast, the guest who arrived at the wedding feast in the parable in Matthew 22:1-14, came there without a wedding garment. As a result of his lack of proper preparation for such an important event, he is also consigned to *"outer darkness."*

OUTER DARKNESS – CHRISTIANS

The final time Jesus uses the term *"outer darkness"* is in His sermon on the Mount of Olives, also known as the Olivet Discourse, that can be found in Matthew 25:14-30. In this portion of His sermon, Jesus used the parable of the talents to show the distinction between the faithful and unfaithful Christian.

> *"And I was afraid, and went and hid thy talent in the earth: lo, there thou hast that is thine. His lord answered and said unto him, Thou wicked and slothful servant, thou knewest that I reap where I sowed not, and gather where I have not strawed: Thou oughtest therefore to have put my money to the exchangers, and then at my coming I should have received mine own with usury. Take therefore the talent from him, and give it unto him which hath ten talents. For unto every one that hath shall be given, and he shall have abundance: but from him that hath not shall be taken away even that which he hath. And cast ye the unprofitable servant into **outer darkness**: there shall be weeping and gnashing of teeth."* (Matthew 25:25-30)

Jesus had given three individuals talents to use. One received 5, the other received 2, and the third received 1 talent. The first two individuals were faithful and were able to double the talents that had been given to them. The third individual was called *"wicked and slothful"* because he buried his talent in the ground. Because of his unfaithfulness, this individual was cast into *"outer darkness"* as well. It is important to understand that the parable of the talents is addressing Christians. Many try to interpret this parable to say Jesus was referring to non-believers, however, the entire context of this parable is to believers.[3]

In his book: **Pictures and Parables**, G.H. Lang shares an experience that expresses an excellent analogy of the term *"outer darkness:"*

> "A too little considered feature of the three references to "outer darkness" is that each pictures a house of feasting...When it is remembered that in the East such a festivity usually took place at night. Staying in a native quarter in Alexandria I was the other side of the road from a large Oriental mansion. One night the whole house was brilliantly lit, a blaze of light from every room, evidently for some special affair. By contrast the street outside and garden around were in black darkness, and nothing further was required to correspond to the term "the darkness the outer," which term equals the darkness which is without, outside the house.
>
> It is outside the Kingdom of heaven when pictured as the temporary festivity at the return of the Lord of the house or as the wedding feast of the son of the house. It is marked by loss of liberty (bound hand and foot), by forfeiture of privilege (the "joy of the lord"), by decrease of knowledge (the pound withdrawn)...It will be healthful that these solemn elements weigh upon our minds and warn and stimulate, though where and how the realities they picture will be experienced may not be known."[4]

While Lang's experience of viewing the Oriental mansion is an analogy of what *"outer darkness"* may be, he properly notes that the reality of what "outer darkness" will actually be like is not known for certain.

(The reader is encouraged to visit the recommended books and websites listed in the **Reference Section** of this book for further study of this important subject).

LOSS OF REWARD

It is important to point out that being assigned to *"outer darkness"* is not punishment for sin, but it does represent the loss of reward for the believer. The Christian will still be with God in eternity, but loses the opportunity of being able to rule and reign with Christ for the 1,000 years.

Also, it is essential to understand that the terms *"kingdom"* and *"outer darkness"* do not represent physical places as such. Instead, the terms *"kingdom"* and *"outer darkness"* represent positions held by the individual involved. In other words, to enter into the Kingdom means that a person enters into a position of ruling and reigning with Christ. The word *"kingdom"* literally means king's dominion, so it refers to the rule of the heavens over the earth. The term *"kingdom"* is not a specific place one would find on a map, but rather an important position of authority that is given to faithful Christians.

Likewise, to be cast into *"outer darkness"* means that the Christian fails to enter into an important position of authority where they rule and reign with Christ for 1,000 years. Since the *"kingdom"* is not a place, *"outer darkness"* is also not a place. Both are expressions of positions where the faithful will rule and reign with Christ, and the unfaithful will not. The unfaithful will experience *"...weeping and gnashing of teeth"* (Matthew 25:30) for 1,000 years while the faithful will experience the delight of the Lord enjoying the blessings of the Messiah's Kingdom.

Outer darkness has been misunderstood by most in the Church because the doctrines of grace and rewards have been misinterpreted. In the chapter that follows, we will look into the subject of "hell," which is another subject that has caused much confusion for many in the Church.

Chapter 7 - Hell

The subject of "hell" is greatly misunderstood by many in the Church today. This misunderstanding has been fostered by years of Traditions that have been handed down from one generation to the next. Properly understanding what hell is requires a great deal of time and study of the Word of God. Unfortunately the Bible does not use one word to describe hell. Instead, the student of the Word of God will find that four different terms are used for Hell:

SHEOL

In the Old Testament the word "Sheol" is used to describe hell. Sheol is used 31 times[5] in the Old Testament and Strong's gives the following description of this word:

> SHEOL (Strong's # 7585)
> "1) sheol, underworld, grave, hell, pit a) the underworld
> b) Sheol-the OT designation for the abode of the dead
> 1) place of no return   2) without praise of God
> 3) wicked sent there for punishment   4) righteous not
>   abandoned to it 5) of the place of exile (fig)
> 6) of extreme degradation in sin"

Sheol is a place. It is the Old Testament term for the abode of the dead.

HADES

In the New Testament, one of the primary words used to describe hell is: "Hades." Hades is the New Testament equivalent of "Sheol" in the Old Testament. Hades is also a place and it is used ten times[6] in the New Testament. Strong's definition for this word is:

HADES (Strong's # 86)
"1) name Hades or Pluto, the god of the lower regions
2) Orcus, the nether world, the realm of the dead
3) later use of this word: the grave, death, hell

In Biblical Greek it is associated with Orcus, the infernal regions, a dark and dismal place in the very depths of the earth, the common receptacle of disembodied spirits. Usually Hades is just the abode of the wicked..."

Both Sheol and Hades are used to describe an actual place. To complicate things further, this place is actually divided into three compartments:

1) Tartarus
2) The Place of Torment (Luke 16:28)
3) Abraham's Bosom (Luke 16:22)

TARTARUS

Tartarus is found one time in the New Testament:

*"For if God spared not the angels that sinned, but cast them down to **hell,** and delivered them into chains of darkness, to be reserved unto judgement;"* (II Peter 2:4)

TARTARUS (Strong's # 5020)
The deepest abyss of Hades: to incarcerate in eternal torment: - cast down to hell. The name of the subterranean region, doleful and dark, regarded by the ancient Greeks as the abode of the wicked dead, where they suffer punishment for their evil deeds.

Tartarus is the place where God cast Lucifer and the fallen angels, which is also referred to in the book of Revelation as the "bottomless pit."[7] Since it is called the bottomless pit, it is probably at the very center of the earth because at that location, the only direction would be up.

Please see the story in Luke 16:19-31[8] for a good description of the place of torment and Abraham's bosom. The place of torment is the place where all who have not been born again will reside until the Great White Throne Judgement. Abraham's bosom is where the elect of God went before the Lord's resurrection. Jesus referred to this place as Paradise when he promised the thief on the cross to take him there. After the resurrection, Jesus transferred Paradise to heaven:

> *"Wherefore he saith, When he ascended up on high, he led captivity captive, and gave gifts unto men. (Now that he ascended, what is it but that he also descended first into the lower parts of the earth? He that descended is the same also that ascended up far above all heavens, that he might fill all things.)"*
> (Ephesians 4:8-10)

Prior to the resurrection, the elect of God went to Abraham's bosom (or Paradise). After the Lord conquered death, he led all those from the lower parts of the earth to heaven.

GEHENNA

The final word that is used for hell in the Bible is the word *"Gehenna."* Gehenna is found 12 times in the New Testament. Unfortunately, the Greek word *"Gehenna"* was mistranslated as hell. Most of the confusion regarding **hell** in the New Testament has been caused by this error made by the translators.

GEHENNA (Strong's # 1067)

> "Valley of hinnon; Gehenna, a valley of Jerusalem, used (figuratively) as a name for the place (or state) of punishment."

The origin of this word relates to a valley outside the city of Jerusalem that was in reality a garbage dump that was constantly kept burning to destroy the filthy debris. Remember, Hades is the New Testament word used for Hell. Gehenna should not have been translated as Hell. By equating these two words with Hell, readers have erroneously thought that Christians could lose their salvation, since Jesus used this term relating to believers in His Sermon on the Mount. This has created much confusion surrounding hell that can be cleared up with a proper understanding of this term, and where it is used in the New Testament.

GEHENNA FOR CHRISTIANS

Most of the uses of the term Gehenna were during the Lord's Sermon on the Mount. Jesus used the term Gehenna to show the severe punishment that would be rendered to those **believers** who were found guilty of gross sins (not confessed and repented of as in I John 1:9 and II Peter 3:9), or for failure to stand up for Christ before men's courts. James used Gehenna in relation to the tongue:

Matthew 5:22	Anger
Matthew 5:29	Adultery - Eye[a]
Matthew 5:30	Adultery - Hand
Matthew 18:9	Offences – Eye
Mark 9:43	Offences – Hand
Mark 9:45	Offences – Foot
Mark 9:47	Offences – Eye
Matthew 10:28	Before Courts – Kill the body
Luke 12:5	Kill the body
James 3:6	Tongue – Potential evil possible

[9]Recommend that Christians read / study each reference.
a) Jesus said looking with lust is equivalent to adultery.

It needs to be remembered that when Christians appear before the Judgement Seat of Christ, our lives will be judged:

> *"For **we must all appear before the judgement seat of Christ**; that every one may receive the things done in his body, according to that he hath done, whether it be **good or bad**."* (II Corinthians 5:10)

Also, both the good and bad that we do will be **judged by fire**:

> *"Now if any man build upon this foundation gold, silver, precious stones, wood, hay, stubble; Every man's work shall be made manifest: for the day shall declare it, because it shall be revealed by fire; and the **fire shall try every man's work** of what sort it is. If any man's work abide which he hath built thereupon, he shall receive a reward. If any man's work shall be burned, he shall suffer loss: but he himself shall be saved; **yet so as by fire.**"* (I Corinthians 3:12-15)

Paul's letter to the Corinthians shows that our works will be tested by **fire** to determine whether they will stand. Works of gold, silver and precious stones will pass through the flames and result in great reward for the believer. However, works of wood, hay and stubble will be destroyed by these same flames. While Paul warns that the believer will suffer loss of reward, he notes they will still be saved.

Remember, the Judgement Seat of Christ will not determine whether or not a person will go to heaven. That determination has already been made at the cross of Calvary. All people who have been born again will go to heaven. The Judgement Seat of Christ will try the works of Christians to determine rewards. The fire used at the Judgement Seat of Christ will test each believer's life to determine either rewards or loss of rewards. Those who arrive at the Judgement Seat of Christ with works of wood, hay and stubble will still be saved, but the **fire** will destroy their works and they will suffer loss as a result.

The fire used at the Judgement Seat of Christ correlates with the same Gehenna fire that Jesus referred to. The Gehenna fire is not Hell, but it does represent the fire that will be used to try and destroy the works and gross sins that were addressed above.

In the previous chapter, we saw that some Christians will not be able to enter into the Kingdom, but will be assigned to "outer darkness" for 1,000 years. Being assigned to *"outer darkness"* represents the loss of reward for the believer. The Christian still goes to heaven, but loses the opportunity of being able to rule and reign with Christ for the 1,000 years.

Similarly, the Christian whose works are destroyed by the Gehenna fire will suffer loss, and thereby lose the opportunity of ruling and reigning with Christ during the Millennium.

GEHENNA FOR JEWS

The last two uses of the term Gehenna are found in Matthew 23:15 and Matthew 23:33.

> *"Woe unto you, scribes and Pharisees, hypocrites! for ye compass sea and land to make one proselyte, and when he is made, ye make him twofold more the child of hell than yourselves."* (Matthew 23:15)
> *"Ye serpents, ye generation of vipers, how can ye escape the damnation of hell?"* (Matthew 23:33)

Jesus used the term Gehenna to address the scribes and Pharisees of His day. The context of this chapter in Matthew is to the religious leader's failure to lead the Jewish people into the truth because of their hypocritical lives.

Apparently, the Lord will judge the Jews in a similar manner in which He will judge the Christians. Jesus uses the term Gehenna to warn both Jews and Christians about their failure to lead faithful lives. This is a severe judgement by fire that will result in great loss. The disobedient Jews and Christians who experience these trying fires will lose their ability of entering into the coming Kingdom and therefore forfeit the ability to rule and reign with Christ for the 1,000 years.

HELLFIRE AND BRIMSTONE

Before we leave the subject of Hell, it seems worth commenting on the preaching style known as the "hellfire and brimstone" preachers. The Baptists are probably most associated with this style of evangelism. While this may not be a popular mainstream approach of preaching, it does have its place in warning the lost about the consequences of rejecting Jesus Christ. As we will see in the next chapter, the lost will have their part in the lake of fire, which is the second death.

However, the fire that we want the Church to understand is the Gehenna fire that will be used at the Judgement Seat of Christ to try the works and gross sins of believers. This is the fire that will be used to test each believer's life to determine either rewards, or loss of rewards.

Christians do not have to worry about the fires of hell, which is reserved for all who have rejected Christ and have not been born again. But Christians do need to be very much concerned about the Gehenna fire that will be used by the Lord to determine our rewards, or lack thereof.

Remember that wood, hay and stubble are destroyed by fire. Also, gross sins that have not been confessed and repented of before one stands at the Judgement Seat of Christ will result in the loss of one's soul. These Christians will still be saved, but the fire will destroy their works and they will not be able to enter into the coming Kingdom. The Gehenna judgement upon the believer is a severe judgement that Christians should fear since it will result in great loss that can still be avoided by repentance.

Because of the mistranslation of Gehenna as hell, preachers have misunderstood what Jesus was trying to convey. Christians cannot go to hell, but some may be in danger of the Gehenna fire when they arrive at the Judgement Seat of Christ.

Chapter 8 – The Second Death

The term *"second death"* is found four times in the book of Revelation. The first instance deals with the lost sinners who have never received Christ as their Savior.

> *"And death and hell were cast into the lake of fire. This is the **second death**."* (Revelation 20:14)

We need to remember that it has been appointed for all men to die once:

> *"And as it is appointed unto men **once to die**, but after this the judgement:"*
> (Hebrews 9:27)

This means that eventually everyone will die once. Living in the endtimes, however, some will be fortunate enough to experience the Rapture and be caught up to the throne of God in a manner similar to the translations of Enoch and Elijah.

But after the appointed first death, Scripture indicates judgement will follow. The *"second death"* mentioned in the above verse in Revelation indicates that all the lost will experience being raised from their state of death to be cast into the lake of fire. In other words, the lost will experience a second death after their lives are judged at the Great White Throne Judgement (Revelation 20:11-14).

This *"second death"* for the lost is being cast into the lake of fire. This is the same place where the Antichrist and the False Prophet will be cast into:

> *"And the beast was taken, and with him the false prophet that wrought miracles before him, with which he deceived them that had received the mark of the*

> *beast, and them that worshipped his image. These both were cast alive into a **lake of fire** burning with brimstone."* (Revelation 19:20)

In addition to the Antichrist and the False Prophet, the adversary the devil, will be cast into the lake of fire:

> *"And the devil that deceived them was cast into the **lake of fire** and brimstone, where the beast and the false prophet are, and shall be tormented day and night for ever and ever."* (Revelation 20:10)

The *"second death"* for the lost means being cast into the lake of fire.

SECOND DEATH FOR CHRISTIANS

Unfortunately, the term *"second death"* is also found in two other places in the book of Revelation that are not related to the lost. The *"second death"* relating to Christians is not understood by most in the Church. Hopefully the explanation that follows will help all believers recognize why this subject is so important to comprehend, and be motivation for them to share with fellow brothers and sisters in Christ.

The usage of *"second death"* relating to Christians can be found in the letter to the Church of Smyrna:

> *"He that hath an ear, let him hear what the Spirit saith unto the churches; He that overcometh shall not be hurt of the **second death**."* (Revelation 2:11)

John is warning Christians in this church. He is saying that those who are *"overcomers"* will not be hurt by the *"second death."* By deduction, this is saying that those who are **not** *overcomers* will be **hurt by** the second death.

The context of this warning to the Christians in Smyrna is the trial of their lives. If they are successful in remaining faithful to Christ by being overcomers, they will be rewarded with the Crown of Life (see Chapter 2):

> *"Fear none of those things which thou shalt suffer: behold, the devil shall cast some of you into prison, that ye may be tried; and ye shall have tribulation ten days: be thou faithful unto death, and I will give thee a crown of life."* (Revelation 2:10)

Those who remain faithful to Christ – by being an overcomer when faced with such a trial – will be rewarded with the Crown of Life, and they will **not be hurt** by the second death. This implies that those who are not successful in being an overcomer will be hurt by the second death.

Remember Jesus said: *"fear him which is able to destroy both* **soul** *and body in* **hell (gehenna).** *"* (Matthew 10:28) These Scriptures are telling us that Christians who are overcomers will not be hurt by the Gehenna fire that will be used to try their lives. The overcomer is successful in saving his soul and will be able to pass through the Gehenna fire at the Judgement Seat of Christ. The reverse holds for those Christians who are not faithful and who are not overcomers. The Gehenna fire at the Judgement Seat of Christ will cause these Christians to lose their soul and thus they will be hurt by the second death. Being hurt by the second death is what John equates with those unfaithful believers who will have their part in the second death:

> *"But the fearful, and unbelieving, and the abominable, and murderers, and whoremongers, and sorcerers, and idolaters, and all liars, shall have their **part in** the lake which burneth with fire and brimstone: which is the* **second death.** *"* (Revelation 21:8)

Being an overcomer is therefore vital for the Christian. Those Christians who are overcomers will save their soul at the Judgement Seat of Christ and gain their entrance into the coming Kingdom. The overcomer is assured that the second death will not hold any power over him. Being an overcomer is such an important subject that an entire chapter will be devoted to it.

SECOND DEATH FOR OLD TESTAMENT SAINTS

The final usage of the term "second death" can be found in Revelation 20:6:

> *"Blessed and holy is he that hath part in the first resurrection: on such the **second death** hath no power, but they shall be priests of God and of Christ, and shall reign with him a thousand years."*

The context to the above passage relates to the first resurrection that will take place after the Second Coming of Christ. John tells us that those who are part of the first resurrection do not have to be concerned with the second death. Because the Old Testament saints are part of the first resurrection they will be able to rule and reign with Christ over the earthly aspect of the coming Kingdom.[10]

SUMMARY

All of the lost people who have rejected Jesus Christ as their Savior will accompany the unholy trio (Satan, Antichrist and the False Prophet) in the lake of fire, which is the second death. The Christian overcomers and those Old Testament saints who are part of the first resurrection will not be affected by the second death. The Christians who fail to be overcomers will be hurt by the second death by losing their souls in the Gehenna fire at the Judgement Seat of Christ.

Chapter 9 – The Book of Life

The term *"book of life"* is found eight times in the New Testament. Once in Philippians 4:3 and seven times in Revelation: 3:5, 13:8, 17:8, 20:12, 20:15, 21:27 and 22:19

All Christians had their names written in the *book of life* from the foundation of the world. This is implied in the following Scripture which shows that all people who are lost will worship the Beast when he rises to power during his 42 month reign of terror on the Earth:

> *"And all that dwell upon the earth shall worship him, whose names are not written in the **book of life** of the Lamb slain from the foundation of the world."*
>
> (Revelation 13:8)

This is saying that Christians who are present during the Tribulation period will not worship the antichrist since all Christians had their names written in the book of life from the foundation of the world.

BLOTTED OUT THE BOOK OF LIFE

The following Scriptures relating to the Church of Sardis indicates that it is possible for some to have their names *blotted out* of the book of life.

> *"4) Thou hast a few names even in Sardis which have not defiled their garments; and they shall walk with me in white: for they are worthy.*
> *5) He that **overcometh**, the same shall be clothed in white raiment; and I will **not blot out his name out of the book of life**, but I will confess his name before my Father, and before his angels."* (Revelation 3:4-5)

Here we see that the overcomers will not have their names blotted out of the book of life. This is similar to what we discovered in the last chapter regarding the overcomers in the Church of Smyrna:

> "He that hath an ear, let him hear what the Spirit saith unto the churches; He that **overcometh** shall not be hurt of the **second death**." (Revelation 2:11)

The overcomers in Smyrna are not hurt by the second death, and the overcomers in Sardis will not have their names blotted out of the book of life.

By implication, those Christians who are not overcomers can be hurt by the second death as we saw in the last chapter. And now we can see, again by implication, that those Christians who are not overcomers can have their names blotted out of the book of life.

SALVATION BY GRACE

We need to remember that we are saved by grace and once we are saved we cannot be lost. However, the above Scripture in Revelation 3:5, is saying that the non-overcoming Christian can have his name blotted out of the book of life. How is this possible?

First, let's look into the meaning of the Greek words used for blot out (Strong's #1813):

1) to anoint or wash in every part
a) to besmear: i.e., **cover with lime (to whitewash or plaster)**
2) to wipe off, wipe away
a) to obliterate, erase, wipe out, blot out

From this we can see that to blot out can be saying that the names are covered over or whitewashed, as in covering with lime or plaster.

In other words, those Christians who are not successful in being overcomers can have their names covered over (as with whitewash) in the book of life. This means that these Christians were not successful in saving their soul because their works were found lacking and they failed to be overcomers.

Remember we are saved by Grace, but our rewards are according to works. The above Scripture (Rev. 3:5) relates the *book of life* to the **works** of the Christian. Interestingly, works will also be used by God at the Great White Throne Judgement:

> *"And I saw a great white throne, and him that sat on it, from whose face the earth and the heaven fled away; and there was found no place for them. And I saw the dead, small and great, stand before God; and the books were opened: and another book was opened, which is the **book of life**: and the dead were judged out of those things which were written in the books, **according to their works**."*
> (Revelation 20:11-12)

From this we can see that the book of life is related to works. When the unsaved appear before the Great White Throne Judgement at the end of the Millennium, they will be judged by their works. This judgement will not be to determine reward, however, the works of the unsaved will be used to determine the level of punishment that each will receive.

At the very end of this Great White Throne Judgement it says:

> *"And whosoever was not found written in the book of life was cast into the lake of fire."* (Revelation 20:15)

At the very end of the Millennium after the Great White Throne Judgement it says that if a person's name is not found written in the book of life then they will be cast into the lake of fire. All lost individuals who have not received Christ as their personal Saviour will be sent to the lake of fire.

By implication, the above verse appears to say that there will be some whose names **are** found written in the *book of life*. This seems to imply that the ones whose names are in the book of life must be the Christians whose names had been previously blotted out of the book of life at the very beginning of the Millennium.

The Christians who failed to be overcomers would have lost their souls at the Judgement Seat of Christ and had their names blotted out of the book of life because their works had been found lacking. Their spirits were saved by the precious blood of Jesus Christ, however, their souls were lost because they failed to be overcomers. Their names were blotted out of the book of life, but at the end of the Millennium they are **not** sent to the lake of fire, because their names were written in the book of life from the foundation of the world.

At that point, God will *"wipe away all tears from their eyes"* (Revelation 21:4) for their failure to be part of ruling and reigning with Christ during the Millennial Kingdom, and they will be allowed to enter the new Jerusalem:

> *"And there shall in no wise enter into it any thing that defileth, neither whatsoever worketh abomination, or maketh a lie: but they which are written in the Lamb's **book of life**."* (Revelation 21:27)

All Christians have their name written in the book of life from the foundation of the world and they will ultimately be able to enter into the new Jerusalem.

Chapter 10 – Overcomers

In the last two chapters we have seen the negative consequences for those Christians who are not "Overcomers." Those Christians in the Church in Smyrna who were not overcomers were *"hurt by the second death"* (Chapter 8), while those Christians in the Church of Sardis who were not overcomers were *"blotted out of the book of life"* (Chapter 9).

Most Christians in today's Church have been taught that if they accept Jesus Christ as their Saviour then they are automatically overcomers. Unfortunately, this is not completely true. Granted, accepting Christ is vital to becoming an overcomer, but it is really only the first step.

OVERCOMETH THE WORLD

> *"For whatsoever is born of God overcometh the world: and this is the victory that overcometh the world, even our faith. Who is he that overcometh the world, but he that believeth that Jesus is the Son of God?*
>
> (I John 5:4-5)

The first two times the word *"overcometh"* is used is found in the above Scripture. John is telling us that only those who are born of God, and believe that Jesus is the Son of God, have overcome the world by their faith. All that is required to overcome the world is the Christian's faith in Jesus Christ.

OVERCOMETH THE FLESH & THE DEVIL

But to be considered a successful overcomer at the Judgement Seat of Christ, the Christian also must also be able to overcome the flesh and overcome the devil.

> *"For all that is in the world, the lust of the flesh, and the lust of the eyes, and the pride of life, is not of the Father, but is of the world."* (I John 2:16)

> *"For we wrestle not against flesh and blood, but against principalities, against powers, against the rulers of the darkness of this world, against spiritual wickedness in high places."* (Ephesians 6:12)

Once a person receives Christ as their personal Saviour, they overcome the world by their faith in Jesus. At this point, the battle begins for the believer's soul (see Chapter 3). The flesh wants to gratify itself and the carnal nature will attempt to destroy the new Christian's soul. Remember, the whole goal of our faith is the salvation of our soul:

> *"Receiving the end of your faith, even the **salvation of your souls.**"* (I Peter 1:9)

In order to be a successful overcomer at the Judgement Seat of Christ, the Christian needs to ensure his soul is saved by winning the victory over his flesh and the carnal nature. Only once all three are defeated (the world, the flesh and the carnal nature), will the Christian be considered a true overcomer. This requires a daily victory that won't end until life's journey is complete.

MOTIVATION TO BE AN OVERCOMER

So far we have only looked at two of the seven Churches in the book of Revelation that received negative consequences for their inability to be overcomers. Let's turn our attention now to the many wonderful rewards that can be obtained by those Christians who are successful in becoming true overcomers.

The book of Revelation uses the term *"overcometh"* six more times. The first five times are to the remaining 5 Churches with the last reference in the second-to-last chapter of the entire book.

REWARDS FOR OVERCOMERS

*"He that hath an ear, let him hear what the Spirit saith unto the churches; To him that **overcometh** will I give to **eat of the tree of life,** which is in the midst of the paradise of God.* (Rev. 2:7)

*"He that hath an ear, let him hear what the Spirit saith unto the churches; To him that **overcometh** will I give to **eat of** the **hidden manna**, and will give him a **white stone,** and in the stone a **new name** written, which no man knoweth saving he that receiveth it."* (Rev. 2:17)

*"And he that **overcometh**, and keepeth my works unto the end, to him will I give **power over the nations"*** (Rev. 2:26)

*"Him that **overcometh** will I make a **pillar in the temple** of my God, and he shall go no more out: and I will write upon him the **name of my God**, and the **name of the city** of my God, which is new Jerusalem, which cometh down out of heaven from my God: and I will write upon him **my new name.*** (Rev. 3:12)

*"To him that **overcometh** will I grant to **sit with me in my throne,** even as I also overcame, and am set down with my Father in his throne.* (Rev. 3:21)

*"He that **overcometh** shall **inherit all things**; and I will be his God, and he shall be my son."* (Rev. 21:7)

It is essential for all Christians to comprehend what the above Scriptures are promising to those who are overcomers. The God of the Universe is offering astonishing and fantastic rewards for successfully overcoming the world, the flesh and the devil.

Christians who are able to succeed in overcoming will be granted rewards that are beyond the comprehension of our mortal minds.   Remember that the front cover of this book shows a picture of our Milky Way, and that our solar system is only one tiny segment of this vast galaxy. And the Milky Way is only one galaxy in a Universe with billions of galaxies.

Jesus is offering Christians the incredible ability to sit with Him on His throne and be given the authority to rule the nations. The God of our immense Universe is giving us privileges almost beyond belief. If the Church of Jesus Christ would grasp these incredible Scriptures it could be transformed.

With such outstanding opportunities that will be awarded to those who are able to be overcomers, how can Christians make certain they are successful?

BEING AN OVERCOMER

Being an overcomer is what being a Christian is all about. Learning to be an overcomer can take a lifetime of tests and trials that the Lord uses to discover what a believer is really made of. While myriads of books should have been written on this important subject, only a few modern Christian authors have illuminated the Scriptures that are so vital for the modern Church to know and understand.

It is beyond the scope of this short study to investigate all of the details of being an overcomer. The purpose of this book has been to alert the Church to the importance of the Kingdom in the hope that readers will begin their own exploration of the Scriptures that will ultimately lead them into a life of faithfulness and obedience. To help the reader on this journey it is important to realize that being an overcomer can only be accomplished by the supernatural power of God in the Christian's life. Being an overcomer cannot be achieved by will power or the strength of the individual's flesh. To be an overcomer, the Christian will learn that this supernatural power is manifested in their life by three primary means.

OVERCOMING BY CROSS

The cross of Jesus Christ represents the entire basis of our faith. It represents the death, pain and suffering that Jesus endured for us. Jesus obtained the victory on the cross, and to be an overcoming Christian, we must be willing to suffer for His sake and learn to die to self.

> *"I am **crucified with Christ**: nevertheless I live; yet not I, but Christ liveth in me: and the life which I now live in the flesh I live by the faith of the Son of God, who loved me, and gave himself for me."* (Galatians 2:20)

> *"And they that are Christ's have **crucified the flesh** with the affections and lusts."* (Galatians 5:24)

As Christians, we must learn the lesson that Paul is teaching the Church of Galatia. Only by experiencing the death to our flesh will allow the supernatural power of Christ's victory on the cross to become our victory. By allowing His life to take over our lives we can – and will – experience His overcoming power.

OVERCOMING BY WORD

When Jesus was tempted by Satan, He used the Word of God to overcome his three tests (Matthew 4:4-10).[11]

> But he answered and said, **It is written**, Man shall not live by bread alone, but by every word that proceedeth out of the mouth of God. (Matthew 4:4)

> *Jesus said unto him, **It is written** again, Thou shalt not tempt the Lord thy God.* (Matthew 4:7)

> *Then saith Jesus unto him, Get thee hence, Satan: for **it is written,** Thou shalt worship the Lord thy God, and him only shalt thou serve.* (Matthew 4:10)

Here Jesus showed us that we can use the Word of God to overcome the adversaries' tests. He teaches us that we are to live by the Word (every word out of the mouth of God), to not allow the adversary to ensnare us into foolish tests, and finally to worship and serve the Lord and not be captivated by the adversaries' alluring offers. Jesus used the Word of God to defeat Satan and the overcomer can use this same tool to win their own victory over the adversary.

In addition to our Lord's example of overcoming Satan by the Word of God, the Apostle Paul reminds us:

> *"For the **word of God** is quick, and powerful, and sharper than any twoedged sword, piercing even to the dividing asunder of soul and spirit, and of the joints and marrow, and is a discerner of the thoughts and intents of the heart."* (Hebrews 4:12)

The Christian can only learn to be an overcomer by immersion in the Word of God. God will then use the time the Christian spends to teach and reveal things necessary for us to grow and become the overcomer God wants us to be. Spending time in the Word of God is vital to becoming an overcomer.

OVERCOMING BY SPIRIT

The final means of overcoming the world, the flesh and the adversary is by the supernatural power of the Spirit of God:

> *"Then he answered and spake unto me, saying, This is the word of the LORD unto Zerubbabel, saying, Not by might, nor by power, but **by my spirit**, saith the LORD of hosts."* (Zechariah 4:6)

> *"This I say then, **Walk in the Spirit**, and ye shall not fulfill the lust of the flesh."* (Galatians 5:16)

> *"There is therefore now no condemnation to them which are in Christ Jesus, who walk not after the flesh, but after **the Spirit**."* (Romans 8:1)

In order to be an overcomer, the Christian needs to allow the Spirit of God to control their daily activities. Remember from Chapter 3, that all Christians have the three parts: spirit, soul and body (I Thessalonians 5:23).

Once a person is born again, the Holy Spirit takes up residence in the believer. To be an overcomer, the Christian must permit the Holy Spirit to take charge. The carnal nature and the person's flesh will resist and fight against the wishes of the Holy Spirit, and being an overcomer will only take place if the Holy Spirit is allowed dominion. The victory over the flesh can only be achieved by the supernatural power of God's Spirit. God wants all Christians to experience the sweet victory that is brought about by walking in the Spirit, and being filled with the Spirit, as He directs and empowers our daily walk.

EXAMPLES FROM THE SEVEN CHURCHES

Before we leave the subject of being an overcomer, it is important for us to remember the examples given in the seven Churches in the book of Revelation. These teach important lessons that are prerequisites to being an overcomer.

Ephesus

*"Remember therefore from whence thou art fallen, and **repent**, and do the first works ("first love"- NIV); or else I will come unto thee quickly, and will remove thy candlestick out of his place, except thou repent."*
(Revelation 2:5)

Smyrna

*"Fear none of those things which thou shalt suffer: behold, the devil shall cast some of you into prison, that ye may be tried; and ye shall have tribulation ten days: **be thou faithful unto death**, and I will give thee a crown of life."* (Revelation 2:10)

Pergamos

*"**Repent**; or else I will come unto thee quickly, and will fight against them with the sword of my mouth."*
(Revelation 2:16)

Thyatira

*"But that which ye have already **hold fast** till I come."*
(Revelation 2:25)

Sardis

*" **Be watchful**, and **strengthen the things which remain**, that are ready to die: for I have not found thy works perfect before God."* (Revelation 3:2)

Philadelphia

*"Behold, I come quickly: **hold that fast which thou hast**, that no man take thy crown."* (Revelation 3:11)

Laodicea

*"As many as I love, I rebuke and chasten: be zealous therefore, and **repent**."* (Revelation 3:19)

The above admonitions by our Lord require little commentary. Jesus is instructing the 7 Churches on what is needed for them to become overcomers. May we all meditate on these passages as reminders of areas in our lives that may require our attention for any necessary correction and repentance (I John 1:9).

Chapter 11 – Enter the Kingdom

PRIZE OF THE KINGDOM

"Do you not know that in a race all the runners run, but only one gets the prize? **Run in such a way as to get the prize.** *Everyone who competes in the games goes into strict training. They do it to get a crown that will not last; but we do it to get a crown that will last forever."*
"Therefore I do not run like a man running aimlessly; I do not fight like a man beating the air. No, I beat my body and make it my slave so that after I have preached to others, I myself will not be disqualified for the prize."
(I Corinthians 9:24-27 – NIV).

The great Apostle Paul was sure his spirit was saved, but he also knew that he had to work at saving his soul. He knew that even though he preached to others, he could be disqualified for the prize if he didn't measure up. He knew that he had to work at saving his soul as a runner in a race for a prize. The prize the believer is racing for is a crown that will last forever.

In Chapter 2 we saw the five different crowns. It is highly probable that these crowns are part of what Paul was referring to as the prize. He knew he could be disqualified for the prize, and Jesus warned us in Revelation 3:11: *"Behold, I come quickly: hold that fast which thou hast, that no man take thy crown."*

The prize Paul referred to and the crown Jesus talked about are obtained by works after a person is saved. They represent the rewards faithful and wise believers will receive for their obedience to the Word of God and their devotion to Jesus. They also represent the salvation of the soul and entrance into the

Kingdom as outlined in this book and also seen in the following verse:

> *"Confirming the souls of the disciples, and exhorting them to continue in the faith, and that we must **through much tribulation enter into the kingdom of God.**"*
>
> (Acts 14:22)

Once a person is saved, the number one priority should be seeking entrance into the Kingdom through the salvation of their soul. The prize for winning the race is the salvation of the soul, which is represented by the crowns that are given as a reward for faithful service.

They will be gained only after the trials and tribulations of life are overcome and the righteousness of God has won over the lusts of this dying earthly kingdom. Those Christians who are successful in being overcomers will be rewarded at the Judgement Seat of Christ with the magnificent prize of entering into the coming Kingdom.

The salvation of the soul and entrance into the coming Kingdom are only through much testing and the trial of one's faith. If you are going through difficulty, then REJOICE:

> *"Blessed is the man who **perseveres under trial**, because when he has stood the test, he will receive the **crown of life** that God has promised to those who love Him."*
>
> (James 1:12 – NIV)

The Lord uses the test and trials of this life to determine who will be qualified to enter the coming Kingdom. By persevering in this life, the Christian will be richly rewarded with the *prize*, which represents gaining entrance into the coming Kingdom and the ability to rule and reign with Jesus Christ!

BORN OF WATER AND THE SPIRIT

Remember, Jesus said that we must be born again to see the coming Kingdom, but He also gave the following requirement for entering into the Kingdom:

> *"Jesus answered, Verily, verily, I say unto thee, Except a man be **born of water** and of the Spirit, he cannot **enter into the kingdom of God.**"* (John 3:5)

Being *"born of water"* means that the believer has been sanctified by the *"washing of water by the word":*

> *"Husbands, love your wives, even as Christ also loved the church, and gave himself for it; That he might **sanctify** and cleanse it with **the washing of water by the word,"*** (Ephesians 5:25-26)

In order to enter into the coming Kingdom, the Christian must allow the Word of God to sanctify and cleanse their life. Remember, the overcomers rely upon the supernatural power of the Cross, the Spirit, and the Word in order to obtain their victory over the world, the flesh and the devil. Sanctification by the Word of God is one of the key ingredients employed in becoming an overcomer. By spending time reading the Word, the Christian receives the sanctification of their soul (please see Hebrews 4:12 and James 1:21), and the supernatural power to overcome whatever tests and trials they may face. (Also, please see: www.prophecycountdown.com/books/the-kingdom/ for a *Supplemental Article* that discusses: *"Born of Water."*)

LAW OF CHRIST

Under the Old Testament, people had the Law of God that they were required to keep. Failure to keep the law would ultimately result in death and separation from God.

Under the New Testament, the Christian is no longer required to keep the Law of God for salvation since it is provided by the grace of God through faith in the atoning sacrifice of Jesus Christ. Faith in Christ is all that is required for salvation.

However, the New Testament also introduced the law of Christ:

> "Bear ye one another's burdens, and so fulfill the **law of Christ**." (Galatians 6:2)

Here the Apostle Paul was referring to the New Testament law that Jesus gave. Paul knew that we are saved by grace:

> "For by grace are ye saved through faith; and that not of yourselves: it is the gift of God: Not of works, lest any man should boast."
> (Ephesians 2:8-9)

The new requirement that Paul was referring to in his letter to the Church of Galatia was the *"law of Christ."* The law of Christ refers to the new requirements that Jesus gave in His Sermon on the Mount that can be found in Matthew 5-7. This entire sermon represents Christ's teachings (law of Christ) that need to be followed for the believer to gain their own entrance into the coming Kingdom:

> "But **seek ye first the kingdom** of God, and his righteousness; and all these things shall be added unto you." (Matthew 6:33)

Robert Govett says in his book: ***Kingdom of God Future***:[12]

> "...in the Sermon on the Mount...He was teaching those who would listen, the principles which were to guide their conduct, **if they would enter the millennial Kingdom**....New principles of far greater height and

depth than the old ones of the Law are in the Sermon on the Mount disclosed by Jesus. They were God's words put into His mouth. While they were "sayings of mine," as He says; they were still "the will of His Father in heaven."

The Sermon on the Mount represents the new *"law of Christ"* that God gave to Christians to help them gain their own entrance into the coming Kingdom. As Govett points out, His sermon had new principles of far greater height and depth. These principles are not necessary for salvation, which is provided as a free gift, but they are required if the believer wants to enter into the millennial Kingdom.

In our Lord's farewell address before He left this planet, Jesus gave us the great commission:

> *"Go ye therefore, and teach all nations, baptizing them in the name of the Father, and of the Son, and of the Holy Ghost:* **Teaching them to observe all things whatsoever I have commanded you***: and, lo, I am with you always, even unto the end of the world. Amen."*
>
> (Matthew 28:19-20)

What many fail to realize about the great commission is the fact that Jesus was telling us that we should be teaching people to observe (do) all of the things He had told us about. The Sermon on the Mount should certainly be included in what Christians need to observe.

In the Sermon on the Mount,[13] Jesus was not teaching people on what they need to do in order to be saved, He was teaching Christians on the principles that they need to follow in order to enter into the Kingdom. (The reader is encouraged to read Matthew 5-7 + Footnote[13]).

SEEK FIRST THE KINGDOM

As outlined above, our Lord told us we should: *"Seek first the Kingdom of God..."* In this hectic, fast-paced time in which we live most of humanity is preoccupied with all too many other obsessions to care about the Kingdom of God. Even today's modern Church is engrossed in the many programs and activities that have been developed to increase attendance, or to reach more "souls" for Jesus Christ.

Bringing more people to the Lord is a wonderful agenda to have, however, Christians need to realize that coming to Christ is only part of the great commission. The part that is missing from most Churches today is teaching believers about *"entering into the Kingdom."* Most Churches do a wonderful job of evangelism and leading people to salvation in Christ. However, through tradition that has been handed down, most Christians believe they will automatically be included in the coming Kingdom because they have been saved. As this book has pointed out, many Christians will not enter into the coming Kingdom. Due to erroneous teaching, and lack of knowledge of the truth, many Christians will be excluded from ruling and reigning with Christ:

> *"My people are destroyed for lack of knowledge: because thou hast rejected knowledge, I will also reject thee..."* (Hosea 4:6)

MEAT IN DUE SEASON

The material included in this brief study represents *"strong meat"* that is greatly needed by many Christians in our Churches today. We are living in the endtimes and Jesus Christ is getting ready to return very soon. Jesus speaks of the time we are living in and tells us what the faithful and wise will be doing:

> *"Therefore be ye also ready: for in such an hour as ye think not the Son of man cometh. Who then is a faithful and wise servant, whom his lord hath made ruler over his household, to give them **meat in due season**? Blessed is that servant, whom his lord when he cometh shall find so doing. Verily I say unto you, That he shall make him ruler over all his goods."*
>
> (Matthew 24:45-47)

The faithful and wise servants (Christians) will be giving out this important meal of *"meat"* at just the right time before the Lord returns. They are seen actively distributing this meat in order to help others gain their own entrance into the coming Kingdom. Since most of the Church has been on a diet of milk for so long, they will have a hard time accepting and digesting this strong meat. Salvation of the soul and entrance into the Kingdom are not taught in most Churches today, but this vital nourishment is seriously needed if Christians are going to be prepared when Jesus comes.

RULE AND REIGN WITH CHRIST

At the end of the above story about distributing this important meat just before the Lord returns, Jesus tells us that those who are found faithful will be given rule over all of his goods. In other words, those who are found diligently giving out this important information will be given the wonderful opportunity of ruling with Jesus!

Those faithful and wise believers who take this duty seriously will be richly rewarded in the coming Kingdom. But more important than these rewards, the motivation for this should be to please the Lord and to help save the souls of those Christians who are asleep and unaware of these important truths.

> *"But as it is written, Eye hath not seen, nor ear heard, neither have entered into the heart of man, the things which God hath prepared for them that love him."*
>
> (I Corinthians 2:9)

For those Christians who love God and have proven to be faithful servants, God has prepared a future that is far beyond anything that we could ever imagine.

God created the vast Universe, which is only partially depicted in the picture of our Milky Way found on the cover of this book. Since He created all of these things, which are beyond our ability to comprehend, it seems clear that we have little idea of what He has in store. Our God is truly Great, and our eyes, and ears and hearts have never understood what He has planned for those who truly love Him.

We hope this brief study has helped readers understand that the first priority of every believer should be seeking the Kingdom and His righteousness. Seeking the coming Kingdom and our entrance into it should be the passion of every Christian.

LUKEWARM OR NEW BELIEVER

Many believers reading this book may be new Christians, or they may be older believers in the faith who have either backslidden, or have never really grown in the faith. Maybe you are just a lethargic believer, or perhaps you left the Church because of one reason or another. Or perhaps you are a Christian whom Satan has bound by some secret sin or habit and you have not been able to break free. Can you still qualify to enter into the coming Kingdom?

The answer to any and all of the above is a resounding: YES!

Until Jesus Christ returns, the Christian reading this book still has the opportunity to repent and cry out to Jesus for help. A good example of this is found in the story of the thief who died on the cross next to Jesus:

> *"Then one of the criminals who were hanged blasphemed Him, saying, "If You are the Christ, save Yourself and us."* *But the other, answering, rebuked him, saying, "Do you not even fear God, seeing you are under the same condemnation? And we indeed justly, for we receive the due reward of our deeds; but this Man has done nothing wrong." Then he said to Jesus,* ***"Lord, remember me when You come into Your kingdom."*** *And Jesus said to him, "Assuredly, I say to you, today you will be with Me in Paradise."*
>
> (Luke 23:39-43 NKJ)

The second thief on the cross was lost. Just before he died he came to realize who Jesus was. He understood that he deserved to die for the life that he had lived. But he also realized who Jesus was and that He had done nothing wrong. He then acknowledged Jesus as ***"Lord"*** and cried out in his one last prayer before he died: ***"...remember me when You come into Your Kingdom."***

This dying thief was given the assurance by our Lord that He would answer his prayer and allow him to enter into His Kingdom.

If you are reading this book today and the Lord has not returned, there still is hope for you to enter into the Kingdom. Humble yourself before the Lord and cry out for Him to help you live the remainder of your life for Him. Ask Him to guide and direct your life as you seek Him and His coming Kingdom.

If you want to make sure you are ready to enter into the coming Kingdom, why not make the following prayer the prayer of your heart right now:

> *"Dear God in Heaven, I realize that I have not been living my life for you. I humbly turn to you right now and ask you to forgive me. Dear Jesus, please rule and reign in my heart and life. Please help me to live for you for whatever time remains. I pray that I may be able to escape all that is about to happen, and that I may be able to enter into your Kingdom when you return for me. In Jesus' name I pray. Amen"*

Our prayer is that many in the Church will pray this prayer and ask the Lord to help them be counted worthy of the coming Kingdom.

> *"And now, little children, **abide in him**; that, when he shall appear, **we may have confidence**, and not be ashamed before him **at his coming**."* (I John 2:28)

> *"Beloved, now are we the sons of God, and it doth not yet appear what we shall be: but we know that, when he shall appear, we shall be like him; for we shall see him as he is. **And every man that hath this hope in him purifieth himself, even as he is pure.**"* (I John 3:2-3)

And let us never forget the prayer for watchfulness that our Lord instructed us to pray:

*"And take heed to yourselves, lest at any time your hearts be overcharged with surfeiting, and drunkenness, and cares of this life, and so that day come upon you unawares. For as a snare shall it come on all them that dwell on the face of the whole earth. **Watch ye, therefore, and pray always, that ye may be accounted worthy to escape all these things that shall come to pass, and to stand before the Son of man**"* (Luke 21:34-36).

Epilogue

If someone offered you $1 million now, or the opportunity to rule and reign with Jesus Christ on His throne, which would you choose?

Remember that Esau sold his birthright for a morsel of food (Hebrews 12:16-17). He gave up his inheritance for such a trivial object. Is there something that you would exchange for your ability to rule and reign with Jesus Christ?

Hopefully, this brief study has pointed out how really insignificant all the things of this world are in relationship to the opportunity to rule and reign with Christ.

It is our hearts' desire that this book will result in a countless number of Christians receiving numerous rewards when they appear at the Judgement Scat of Christ and be able to rule and reign with Christ in His coming Kingdom.

By faithfully living a life that is pleasing to the Lord, may He find each of us diligently striving to delight Him in order to hear Him say:

> *"Well done, thou good and faithful servant... enter into the joy of thy Lord"* (Matthew 25:21).

ARE YOU READY TO
RULE AND REIGN WITH CHRIST?

"The Spirit and the Bride say, Come..."
(Revelation 22:17)

*"How narrow is the gate and difficult is the way which leads
to life, and there are few who find it."*
(Matthew 7:14 – NKJV)

Reference Notes

Prologue
1) Those readers who are unfamiliar with Kingdom truths are encouraged to read our tract: *Aspects of the Kingdom*:
www.prophecycountdown.com/endtimetracts.php

Chapter 2
2) Pastor Gary Whipple has written an excellent book entitled: **Shock and Surprise Beyond the Rapture**. This author was fortunate to live in the same area where Pastor Whipple led a small congregation where he taught on the Kingdom truths. While we held different views in certain areas concerning his analysis of the separation that will occur at the Rapture, his book is an excellent primer on the Kingdom truths that are rarely found in the local Christian book store. Despite these differences, we highly recommend this book.

Chapter 6
3) Lyn Mize has an excellent study of the Olivet Discourse that can be found on his website:
www.ffruits.org/firstfruits02/olivetdiscourse.html

Lyn does an outstanding job of showing how this important sermon by our Lord has vital information for the Jews, the Gentiles and the Church.

4) G.H. Lang, **Pictures and Parables**, Schoettle Publishing Co., 1985, pp. 306-307. Also see: www.schoettlepublishing.com

Chapter 7
5) **Sheol** is found thirty-one (31) times in the Old Testament:
Deut. 32:22, II Sam. 22:6, Job 11:8, Job 26:6, Psa. 9:17,
Psa. 16:10, Psa. 18:5, Psa. 55:15, Psa. 86:13, Psa. 116:3,
Psa 139:8, Pro. 5:5, Pro. 7:27, Pro. 9:18, Pro. 15:11, Pro. 15:24,
Pro. 23:14, Pro 27:20, Isa. 5:14, Isa. 14:9, Isa 14:15, Isa. 28:18,
Isa. 28:18, Isa. 57:9, Eze. 31:16, Eze. 31:17, Eze 32:21,
Eze 32:27, Amo. 9:2, Jon. 2:2, and Hab. 2:5

6) **Hades** in found ten (10) times in the New Testament: Mat. 11:23, Mat. 16:18, Luk. 10:15, Luk. 16:23, Act 2:27, Act. 2:31, Rev. 1:18, Rev. 6:8. Rev. 20:13 and Rev. 20:14

7) *"Bottomless pit"* is found seven (7) times in Revelation: Revelation 9:1, 9:2, 9:11, 11:7, 17:8, 20:1, and 20:3

8) Luke 16:19-31

*"19) There was a certain rich man, which was clothed in purple and fine linen, and fared sumptuously every day: 20) And there was a certain beggar named Lazarus, which was laid at his gate, full of sores, 21) And desiring to be fed with the crumbs which fell from the rich man's table: moreover the dogs came and licked his sores. 22) And it came to pass, that the beggar died, and was carried by the angels into **Abraham's bosom**: the rich man also died, and was buried; 23) And in hell he lift up his eyes, being in torments, and seeth Abraham afar off, and Lazarus in his bosom. 24) And he cried and said, Father Abraham, have mercy on me, and send Lazarus, that he may dip the tip of his finger in water, and cool my tongue; for I am **tormented in this flame**. 25) But Abraham said, Son, remember that thou in thy lifetime receivedst thy good things, and likewise Lazarus evil things: but now he is comforted, and thou art tormented. 26) And beside all this, between us and you there is a great gulf fixed: so that they which would pass from hence to you cannot; neither can they pass to us that would come from thence. 27) Then he said, I pray thee therefore, father, that thou wouldest send him to my father's house: 28) For I have five brethren; that he may testify unto them, lest they also come into this **place of torment**. 29) Abraham saith unto him, They have Moses and the prophets; let them hear them. 30) And he said, Nay, father Abraham: but if one went unto them*

from the dead, they will repent. 31) And he said unto him, If they hear not Moses and the prophets, neither will they be persuaded, though one rose from the dead. "

9) Scriptures where Gehenna is mistranslated as hell:

"But I say unto you, That whosoever is angry with his brother without a cause shall be in danger of the judgement: and whosoever shall say to his brother, Raca, shall be in danger of the council: but whosoever shall say, Thou fool, shall be in danger of **hell fire** *(Gehenna).* " (Matthew 5:22)

"And if thy right eye offend thee, pluck it out, and cast it from thee: for it is profitable for thee that one of thy members should perish, and not that thy whole body should be cast into **hell** *(Gehenna).* " (Matthew 5:29)

"And if thy right hand offend thee, cut it off, and cast it from thee: for it is profitable for thee that one of thy members should perish, and not [that] thy whole body should be cast into **hell** *(Gehenna).* " (Matthew 5:30)

"And if thine eye offend thee, pluck it out, and cast it from thee: it is better for thee to enter into life with one eye, rather than having two eyes to be cast into **hell fire** *(Gehenna).* "
(Matthew 18:9)

"And if thy hand offend thee, cut it off: it is better for thee to enter into life maimed, than having two hands to go into **hell** *(Gehenna), into the fire that never shall be quenched:* "
(Mark 9:43)

"And if thy foot offend thee, cut it off: it is better for thee to enter halt into life, than having two feet to be cast into **hell** *(Gehenna), into the fire that never shall be quenched:* "
(Mark 9:45)

And if thine eye offend thee, pluck it out: it is better for thee to *enter into the kingdom of God with one eye, than having two eyes to be cast into **hell fire**: (Gehenna)* (Mark 9:47)

*"And fear not them which kill the body, but are not able to kill the soul: but rather fear him which is able to destroy both soul and body in **hell** (Gehenna)."* (Matthew 10:28)

*"But I will forewarn you whom ye shall fear: Fear him, which after he hath killed hath power to cast into **hell** (Gehenna); yea, I say unto you, Fear him."* (Luke 12:5)

*"And the tongue is a fire, a world of iniquity: so is the tongue among our members, that it defileth the whole body, and setteth on fire the course of nature; and it is set on fire of **hell** (Gehenna)."* (James 3:6)

Chapter 8
10) Lyn Mize has an excellent study of Revelation that can be found on his website:

http://www.ffruits.org/firstfruits02/revchp20.html

Part of Lyn's analysis of the first resurrection follows:

> "It is also clear that a resurrection takes place in this chapter, but there is no translation of humans that are alive since the bodies they have are suited for inhabiting the earth. It is also significant that this resurrection is called the first resurrection. This seems inconsistent with the rest of Scripture since we know that those in the Church have already been resurrected. It is important to remember that the Church Age is a parenthetical insertion of an age into God's dealing with the Jews.
>
> At this point in time in this chapter, the Church Age is over and God's determination of those in the Church who will reign in the heavenly aspect of the kingdom has been completed. God is now dealing with the earthly

aspects and this is the first resurrection of those who will enter the earthly aspect of the kingdom. The second resurrection is at the end of the millennium, and it is a resurrection of the unsaved dead of all ages.

The first resurrection in this chapter is the resurrection that the Old Testament saints looked forward to since they knew nothing about the Church Age, and the resurrections for that particular dispensation..."

Chapter 10
11) Matthew 4:3-10:

"*3) And when the tempter came to him, he said, If thou be the Son of God, command that these stones be made bread. 4) But he answered and said, **It is written**, Man shall not live by bread alone, but by every word that proceedeth out of the mouth of God. 5) Then the devil taketh him up into the holy city, and setteth him on a pinnacle of the temple,   6) And saith unto him, If thou be the Son of God, cast thyself down: for it is written, He shall give his angels charge concerning thee: and in their hands they shall bear thee up, lest at any time thou dash thy foot against a stone. 7) Jesus said unto him, **It is written** again, Thou shalt not tempt the Lord thy God.8) Again, the devil taketh him up into an exceeding high mountain, and sheweth him all the kingdoms of the world, and the glory of them;   9)   And saith unto him, All these things will I give thee, if thou wilt fall down and worship me.   10) Then saith Jesus unto him, Get thee hence, Satan: for **it is written,** Thou shalt worship the Lord thy God, and him only shalt thou serve.*"

Chapter 11
12) Robert Govett, ***Kingdom of God Future***, 1985, page 102, Conley & Schoettle Publishing Co., (Originally 1870)

Also, please see: www.schoettlepublishing.com .

13) For an excellent study of the Sermon on the Mount, please
see Lyn Mize's website:
           www.ffruits.org/firstfruits02/sermononthemount.html

As outlined in Chapter 11, in the Sermon on the Mount Jesus
was teaching Christians on the principles needed to enter into
the coming Kingdom. All Disciples of Jesus Christ would do
well to spend time reading and studying this great exegesis by
Lyn. Our Lord lays out the principles that Christians should
follow in order to enter into the Kingdom.

Other Recommended Books and Websites:
In addition to those books cited earlier in these Reference
Notes, the following books and websites are highly
recommended for those Christians who want to learn more
about the deeper Truths found in the Scriptures. If you want to
learn more about being ready to rule and reign with Christ,
spend time reading and studying the following:

The Open Door by Lyn Mize	www.ffruits.org
Worthy of the Kingdom by Tom Finley	www.seekersofchrist.org
Judgment Seat of Christ by D.M. Panton	www.schoettlepublishing.com
The Bride of Christ by Pastor Randy Shupe	www.pastorrandyshupe.com
Reflections of His Image Kingdom, Power & Glory by Nancy Missler	www.kingshighway.org
Rapture – A Reward for Readiness by Dr. Ray Brubaker	www.godsnews.com

Appendix A – Watching for Jesus

"So Christ was once offered to bear the sins of many; ***and unto them that look for him shall he appear the second time*** *without sin unto salvation."* (Hebrews 9:28)

The Word of God says that Jesus is returning the second time to those who are looking for him to return. Are you looking for Jesus to come again? If not, now is the time to start your watch because it is much later than most people think.

We do not know for certain the exact time that Jesus will return. Just before Jesus left this earth the first time he told His disciples that He was going to return and He commanded them to "Watch". What does it mean to continue watching?

Some of the things *"Watching"* entails include:

1) Being aware of the prophetic signs in God's Word.
2) Living a life of Holiness before our Lord.
3) Living a life separated from the world.
4) Encouraging one another with the wonderful Hope of His soon return.
5) Telling others Jesus is coming soon and that they need to be ready.
6) Praying the prayer Jesus taught us to pray in Luke 21:

"And take heed to yourselves, lest at any time your hearts be overcharged with surfeiting, and drunkenness, and cares of this life, and so that day come upon you unawares. For as a snare shall it come on all them that dwell on the face of the whole earth. ***Watch*** *ye, therefore, and* ***pray always****, that ye may be accounted worthy to escape all these things that shall come to pass, and to stand before the Son of man"*
(Luke 21:34-36).

The act of *"Watching"* is serious business with our Lord. If we fail to continue our diligence, Revelation 3:3, gives us fair warning:

> *"Remember therefore how thou hast received and heard, and hold fast, and repent. If therefore **thou shalt not watch**, I will **come on thee as a thief**, and thou **shalt not know** what hour I will come upon thee."*
> (Revelation 3:3)

Those who are not *"Watching"* will be taken by surprise since a thief comes unannounced. The Wise and Faithful followers of Jesus, however, will continue *"Watching"* for Him and they will not be surprised. Begin *"Watching"* today before it is too late!

In Appendix B that follows, we discuss the incredible **Sign** that Jesus said would announce His soon return. Comet Hale-Bopp arrived on the world scene in 1997, thirty years after the recovery of Old Jerusalem in 1967; per Bullinger's observation of the significance of the number thirty where "30 being 3 x 10, denotes in a higher degree the perfection of Divine order, as **marking the right moment...**"

Hale-Bopp was the most widely viewed comet in the history of mankind, and if the Generation Jesus referred to in Matthew 24 began in 1967, the arrival of Comet Hale-Bopp in 1997 was a Divine marking at just the right moment to let us know where we are in God's prophetic calendar. Indeed, Jesus is Coming, Very, Very Soon!

Please visit our Website: www.ProphecyCountdown.com for any possible: *News Updates* or *Supplemental Articles* on the Kingdom Tab of the website to help you continue in your personal *"Watch"* and preparation for the coming Kingdom.

Appendix B

Sign of Christ's Coming

April 8, 1997

Comet Hale-Bopp Over New York City
Credit and Copyright: J. Sivo
http://antwrp.gsfc.nasa.gov/apod/ap970408.html

"What's that point of light above the World Trade Center? It's Comet Hale-Bopp! Both faster than a speeding bullet and able to "leap" tall buildings in its single orbit, Comet Hale-Bopp is also bright enough to be seen even over the glowing lights of one of the world's premier cities. In the foreground lies the East River, while much of New York City's Lower Manhattan can be seen between the river and the comet."

"As it was in the days of Noah, so it will be at the coming of the Son of Man." (Matthew 24:37 – NIV)

These words from our wonderful Lord have several applications about the Tribulation period that is about to ensnare this world.

Seas Lifted Up
Throughout the Old Testament, the time of the coming Tribulation period is described as the time when the "seas have lifted up," and also as coming in as a "flood" (please see Jeremiah 51:42, Hosea 5:10, Daniel 11:40 and Psalm 93:3-4 for just a few examples).

This is a direct parallel to the time of Noah when the Great Flood of water came to wipe out every living creature except for righteous Noah and his family, and the pairs of animals God spared. While God said He would never flood the earth again with water, the coming Judgement will be by fire (II Peter 3:10). The book of Revelation shows that approximately three billion people will perish in the terrible time that lies ahead (see Revelation 6:8 and 9:15).

2 Witnesses
A guiding principle of God is to establish a matter based upon the witness of two or more:

> *"...a matter must be established by the testimony of two or three witnesses"* (Deuteronomy 19:15 – NIV)

In 1994, God was able to get the attention of mankind when Comet Shoemaker-Levy crashed into Jupiter on the 9th of Av (on the Jewish calendar). Interestingly, this Comet was named after the "two" witnesses who first discovered it.

In 1995, "two" more astronomers also discovered another comet. It was called Comet Hale-Bopp, and it reached its closest approach to planet Earth on March 23, 1997. It has been labeled as the most widely viewed comet in the history of mankind.

Scientists have determined that Comet Hale-Bopp's orbit brought it to our solar system 4,465 years ago (see Notes 1 and 2 below). In other words, the comet made its appearance near Earth in 1997 and also in 2468 BC. Remarkably, this comet preceded the Great Flood by 120 years! God warned Noah of this in Genesis 6:3:

> *"My Spirit shall not strive with man forever, for he is indeed flesh; yet his days shall be one hundred and twenty years."*

Days of Noah

What does all of this have to do with the Lord's return? Noah was born around 2948 BC, and Genesis 7:11, tells us that the Flood took place when Noah was 600, or in 2348 BC.

Remember, our Lord told us: ***"As it was in the days of Noah, so it will be at the coming of the Son of Man."*** (Matthew 24:37 – NIV)

In the original Greek, it is saying: ***"exactly like"*** it was, so it will be when He comes (see Strong's #5618).

During the days of Noah, Comet Hale-Bopp arrived on the scene as a harbinger of the Great Flood. Just as this same comet appeared before the Flood, could its arrival again in 1997 be a sign that God's final Judgement, also known as the time of Jacob's Trouble, is about to begin?

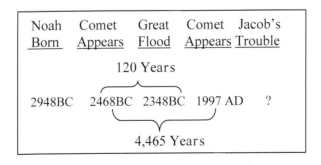

Comet Hale-Bopp's arrived 120 years before the Flood as a warning to mankind. Only righteous Noah heeded God's warning and built the ark, as God instructed. By faith, Noah was obedient to God and, as a result, saved himself and his family from destruction.

Remember, Jesus told us His return would be preceded by great heavenly signs: *"And there shall be signs in the sun, and in the moon, and in the stars; and upon the earth distress of nations, with perplexity; the sea and the waves roaring..."* (Luke 21:25)

Just as this large comet appeared as a 120-year warning to Noah, its arrival in 1997 tells us that Jesus is getting ready to return again. Is this the **"Sign"** Jesus referred to?

Jesus was asked 3 questions by the disciples:
"Tell us, (1) when shall these things be" (the destruction of *the city of Jerusalem),   " and   (2) what shall be the __sign__ of thy coming, and (3) of the end of the world?"* (Matthew 24:3)

Sign of Christ's Coming

The **first** question had to do with events that were fulfilled in 70 AD. The **third** question has to do with the future time at the very end of the age.

The **second** question, however, has to do with the time of Christ's second coming. Jesus answered this second question in His description of the days of Noah found in Matthew 24:33-39:

(33) "So likewise ye, when ye shall see all these things, know that it is near, even at the doors. (34) Verily I say unto you, This generation shall not pass, till all these things be fulfilled. (35) Heaven and earth shall pass away, but my words shall not pass away. (36) But of that day and hour knoweth no man, no, not the angels of heaven, but my Father only. (37) **But as the days of Noe were, so shall also the coming of the Son**

of man be. *(38)For as in the days that were before the flood they were eating and drinking, marrying and giving in marriage, until the day that Noe entered into the ark, (39) And knew not until the flood came, and took them all away; so shall also the coming of the Son of man be."*

Jesus is telling us that the **sign** of His coming will be as it was during the days of Noah. As Comet Hale-Bopp was a sign to the people in Noah's day, its arrival in 1997 is a sign that Jesus is coming back again soon. Comet Hale-Bopp could be the very sign Jesus was referring to, which would announce His return for His faithful.

Remember, Jesus said, *"exactly as it was in the days of Noah, so will it be when He returns."* The appearance of Comet Hale-Bopp in 1997 is a strong indication that the Tribulation period is about to begin, but before then, Jesus is coming for His Bride!

Keep looking up! Jesus is coming again very soon!
As Noah prepared for the destruction God warned him about 120 years before the Flood, Jesus has given mankind a final warning that the Tribulation period is about to begin. The horrible destruction on 9/11 is only a precursor of what is about to take place on planet Earth. We need to be wise like Noah and prepare. Always remember our Lord's instructions:

Watch and Pray
*"(34)And take heed to yourselves, lest at any time your hearts be overcharged with surfeiting, and drunkenness, and cares of this life, and so that day come upon you unawares. (35) For as a snare shall it come on all them that dwell on the face of the whole earth.(36)Watch ye therefore, and **pray always**, that ye may be **accounted worthy to escape all these things that shall come to pass, and to stand before the Son of man"** (Luke 21:34-36).*

Footnotes

(1) The original orbit of Comet Hale-Bopp was calculated to be approximately 265 years by engineer George Sanctuary in his article: **_Three Craters In Israel_**, published on March 31, 2001 that can be found at:
   http://www.gsanctuary.com/3craters.html#3c_r13

Comet Hale-Bopp's orbit around the time of the Flood changed from 265 years to about 4,200 years. Because the plane of the comet's orbit is perpendicular to the earth's orbital plane (ecliptic), Mr. Sanctuary noted: "A negative time increment was used for this simulation…to back the comet away from the earth…. past Jupiter… and then out of the solar system. The simulation suggests that the past-past orbit had a very eccentric orbit with a period of only 265 years. When the comet passed Jupiter (**_around 2203BC_**) its orbit was deflected upward, coming down near the earth 15 months later with the comet's period changed from 265 years to about (**_4,200_**) years." (**_added text_** for clarity)

(2) Don Yeomans, with NASA's Jet Propulsion Laboratory made the following observations regarding the comet's orbit: "By integrating the above orbit forward and backward in time until the comet leaves the planetary system and then referring the osculating orbital elements…the following orbital periods result:
   Original orbital period before entering planetary system = 4200 years. Future orbital period after exiting planetary system = 2380 years."
   This analysis can be found at:
   http://www2.jpl.nasa.gov/comet/ephemjpl6.html

Based upon the above two calculations we have the following:

265 [a] + 4,200 [b] = 4,465 Years

1997 AD – 4,465 Years = 2468 BC = Hale Bopp arrived

(a) Orbit period calculated by George Sanctuary before deflection around 2203 BC.

(b) Orbit period calculated by Don Yeomans after 1997 visit.

Afterword

While the manuscript for this book was completed in August 2009, little did I know that the Lord had more that He wanted me to write.

Once the draft manuscript was completed, it was mailed to many of the friends and followers of our ministry that we began back in 1989. To digress a moment, the ministry of **Prophecy Countdown** was born after the failed prediction by Edgar Whisenant that the Lord was going to return in 1988. While the Lord used Edgar to awaken many to the nearness of Christ's return, many believers were discouraged when the Lord did not come for us in 1988, and our ministry was born to encourage those believers to continue watching. The purpose of our ministry has always been to help the believer's heart maintain an inner watchfulness by kindling a fire of faith and hope in Christ and fanning it with facts, biblical truths and world events until the coming of our Lord.

Many of our brothers and sisters in Christ responded to our mailing and encouraged us with their comments which are included in the final book. Also, our good friend Lyn Mize promptly wrote the Foreword to this book, for which we are very grateful. Finally, Tom Finley was kind enough to review the draft and make several excellent suggestions for changes to the final work.

Then, the Lord led several new friends to our ministry in order to help encourage us in this work. One dear sister in the Lord, who is a professional editor, was so very kind to donate her time and labor of love to review and correct the many grammatical errors that were included in the draft manuscript. Thank you, Dana Kababik, for the excellent work you performed.

Once the book had been reviewed and edited, I thought that it was ready for publication. Then on October 3, I learned that our former pastor, Gary Whipple had passed on to be with the Lord on October 2. With Pastor Whipple's passing, the Church has lost a great teacher of the Kingdom truths. Fortunately, through his wonderful books and website his work will live on. Please see: www.beyondtherapture.com.

While attending his funeral, I was privileged to have the opportunity to meet Pastor Whipple's publisher, Dr. Lewis Schoettle, the owner of Schoettle Publishing Company. His company is one of the leading providers of books on the Kingdom truths, and their website has the best collection of essential authors for the serious student of the Kingdom. Please see: www.schoettlepublishing.com.

Dr. Schoettle was very kind to review our manuscript and we are so grateful to have such a learned man check this work. In addition to reading this book, Dr. Schoettle recommended several authors who we were not acquainted with. The two most notable that I believe the Lord wanted me to become familiar with are: Philip Mauro and George N. H. Peters.

PHILIP MAURO (1859-1952)

Philip Mauro was a foremost patent attorney who came to Christ at age 49. He is probably most famous for writing the brief which William Jennings Bryan used to win the famous Tennessee-Scopes trial (evolution in public schools) in 1925. While his work as a lawyer was impressive, the Lord also used his writing talents to communicate teachings from the Bible. While I do not necessarily agree with all of his writings, his book entitled: *God's Pilgrims* is one which I was immediately attracted to. Mr. Mauro does an outstanding job of explaining one of the least understood teachings in the Church today: the salvation of the soul.

While many of the friends of our ministry are familiar with the subject of the salvation of the soul, most in the Church have never even heard about it! Philip Mauro's treatment of this important subject is excellent and vitally needed for all believers to understand. Because of this, we have added a link called *"Salvation of the Soul"* to the Kingdom tab of our website under the heading of Supplemental Articles that can be found at: www.prophecycountdown.com/books/the-kingdom.

Please take the time to read and study this important material. The salvation of the soul was covered in Chapter 3 of this book, and Philip Mauro's examination of this subject is really must reading for the entire Church.

GEORGE N. H. PETERS (1825-1909)

While I believe the Lord wanted me to become acquainted with Philip Mauro, I am convinced that one of the main reasons for meeting Dr. Schoettle was to be introduced to the life and writings of George Peters.

George Peters was a fundamentalist Lutheran preacher from Ohio who was not well accepted among his own Church. Peters broke from the staunch post-millennialists of his denomination and wrote what has become one of the most exhaustive pre-millennial works ever written on the Kingdom of God: *The Theocratic Kingdom.* In this work of 2,175 pages in three volumes Peters says: "the Theocratic Kingdom is the ultimate goal and leading thought of God and His Scriptures, and every Christian should have his heart and mind dedicated to living such a life as to be worthy of inheriting this Kingdom and enjoying the 1,000 year rest God promises to all those who are faithful to His calling."

As mentioned above, Peter's pre-millennialist teaching was not accepted by his Church, and Wittenberg College, where he graduated, also did not accept the pre-millennial position. As a result, his teaching made him fairly obscure when his work was first published in 1883. This impression is noted and keenly felt as he ends the Introduction of his book:

> "May the author add: after many years of labor – as the following pages indicated – **and the cold fraternization of "brethren" who had no sympathy for Chiliastic (pre-millennial) study**, it would be a personal gratification to the writer to learn from students who have investigated the subjects presented in this work, that the perusal of this book has given them pleasure and strengthened them in "the blessed hope."

It appears that George Peter's break from the mainstream theology of the day cost him dearly. He probably lost many friends and colleagues for teaching against accepted beliefs, but he was standing on what he believed the Scriptures to say.

I believe the Lord wanted me to see this because the teachings in this book are not accepted by today's Church. The Laodicean era in which we live does not care to hear about the "salvation of the soul" or "seeking first the Kingdom." Most of the Church may treat my work of *The Kingdom* as many treated Peters. I can only echo his words as I close this book:

> "The doctrine herein advocated, because of its being so directly opposed to the current theology, and perhaps new in form to some reader, must not regard in the light of a novelty. It is, as we shall show, far older than the Christian Church, and was ably advocated by the founders and immediate supporters of that Church."

James T. Harman
10/22/2009

Special Invitation

This book was written to those who have been saved by Jesus Christ. If you have never been saved before, would you like to be saved? The Bible shows that it's simple to be saved...

- Realize you are a sinner.
  "As it is written, There is none righteous, no, not one:" (Romans 3:10)
  "... for there is no difference. For all have sinned, and come short of the glory of God;" (Romans 3:22-23)
- Realize you CAN NOT save yourself.
  "But we are all as an unclean thing, and all our righteousness are as filthy rags; ..." (Isaiah 64:6)
  "Not by works of righteousness which we have done, but according to his mercy he saved us, ..." (Titus 3:5)
- Realize that Jesus Christ died on the cross to pay for your sins.
  "Who his own self bare our sins in his own body on the tree, ..." (I Peter 2:24)
  "... Unto him that loved us, and washed us from our sins in his own blood," (Revelation 1:5)
- Simply by faith receive Jesus Christ as your personal Savior.
  "But as many as received him, to them gave he power to become the sons of God, even to them that believe on his name:" (John 1:12)
  " ...Sirs, what must I do to be saved? And they said, Believe on the Lord Jesus Christ, and thou shalt be saved, and thy house." (Acts 16:30-31)
  "...if you confess with your mouth, 'Jesus is Lord,' and believe in your heart God raised him from the dead, you will be saved." (Romans 10:9 – NIV)

WOULD YOU LIKE TO BE SAVED?

If you want to be saved, you can receive Jesus Christ right now by making the following confession of faith:

> Lord Jesus, I know that I am a sinner, and unless you save me, I am lost forever. I thank you for dying for me at Calvary. By faith I come to you now, Lord, the best way I know how, and ask you to save me. I believe that God raised you from the dead and acknowledge you as my personal Saviour.

If you believed on the Lord, this is the most important decision of your life. You are now saved by the precious blood of Jesus Christ, which was shed for you and your sins. Now that you have received Jesus as your personal Saviour, you will want to find a Church where you can be baptized as your first act of obedience, and where the Word of God is taught so you can continue to grow in your faith. Ask the Holy Spirit to help you as you read the Bible to learn all that God has for your life.

Also, go to the Reference section of this book where you will find recommended books and websites that will help you on your wonderful journey.

Endtimes
The Bible indicates that we are living in the final days and Jesus Christ is getting ready to return very soon. This book was written to help Christians prepare for what lies ahead. The Word of God indicates that the Tribulation Period is rapidly approaching and that the Antichrist is getting ready to emerge on the world scene.

Jesus promised His disciples that there is a way to escape the horrible time of testing and persecution that will soon devastate this planet. The whole purpose of this book is to help you get prepared so you will rule and reign with Jesus when He returns.

About The Author

Jim Harman has been a Christian for over 30 years. He has diligently studied the Word of God with a particular emphasis on Prophecy. Jim has written several books and the three most essential titles are available at www.ProphecyCountdown.com: *The Coming Spiritual Earthquake, Don't Be Left Behind, and The Kingdom;* which have been widely distributed around the world. These books encourage many to continue *"Looking"* for the Lord's soon return, and bring many to a saving knowledge of Jesus Christ.

Jim's professional experience includes being a Certified Public Accountant (CPA) and a Certified Property Manager (CPM). He has an extensive background in both public accounting and financial management with several well known national firms.

Jim has been fortunate to have been acquainted with several mature believers who understand and teach the deeper truths of the Bible. It is Jim's strong desire that many will come to realize the importance of seeking the Kingdom and seeking Christ's righteousness as we approach the soon return of our Lord and Saviour Jesus Christ.

The burden of his heart is to see many believers come to know the joy of Christ's triumph in their life as they become true overcomers; qualified and ready to rule and reign with Christ in the coming Kingdom.

To contact the author for questions or to arrange for speaking engagements

Jim Harman
P.O. Box 941612
Maitland, FL 32794
JimHarmanCPA@aol.com

Reader's Comments

"One Saturday morning in the early 90's, while working in my kitchen, the Lord said, "turn your TV on." Ray Brubaker was on the TBN channel holding up to the camera the book: **"The Coming Spiritual Earthquake"** *by James Harman. Brother Brubaker said, "Every Christian needs to read this book." I immediately ordered it and was so grateful because for several years the Lord had been showing me, "He is a Rewarder of them who diligently seek Him." (Hebrews 11:6) He also led me to writings of other bygone Faithfuls (Panton, Govett, Pember, etc.) who reaffirmed the doctrine of Christ's Coming 1,000 Year Millennial Reign on this Earth and only the Faithful Christians would be there. Jim's new book entitled:* **The Kingdom**, *has laid it all out so plainly that even a child in the faith could understand. If this book has come into your hands, you are blessed of God. May HE continue to give us ears to hear and hearts to fully respond to His gracious invitation to Share His Throne."*
Joan Olsen – Edmond, OK

"Please know that I believe wholeheartedly in your message and have been enriched by your ability to go beneath the mere surface and find the treasures of scriptural truth that fit so cohesively together. Thank You for your endeavor Jim, as your obedience to search out The Word has served to deepen my faith and solidly anchor me in that Blessed Hope. I believe your message is sound and so very timely: "For such a time as this".
Patricia A. Hucko M.A, NCC, LPC – Basking Ridge, NJ

"Eye opening- **The Kingdom** *made me consider things that I've never heard preached or even thought about before. It inspired me to dig deeper into God's word to understand more. My thanks Jim, for sparking my curiosity and helping me on my journey to The Kingdom."* Willie Wilson – Winter Springs, FL

Reader's Comments

*"**The Kingdom** emphasizes one of the most important messages that needs to be trumpeted in these last days . . . that it is absolutely imperative for every believer to cultivate intimacy with Jesus and be the overcoming bride that He is seeking...I highly recommend Jim's book. It really is must reading for every believer."* Daniel Rydstedt – Springfield, MO
Author of the *Be The Bride!* Series

*"Although I strongly disagree with the once-saved--always-saved doctrine, I am recommending that all Christians, because of the extreme lateness of the hour, take the message of this book to heart, as each one of us has so much to lose and so much to gain, FOR ALL ETERNITY. Your book is the type of book that is needed for extra motivation for holiness, complete surrender, service, and seeking the Lord's perfect will for our lives. "**The Kingdom**" is straight to the point, well-written, and a book that all Christians could benefit from, by reading it. Like your other books, one is forced to take a closer look at the Scriptures to see what the future really holds."*
Ron Reese – Brooklyn, MI
Maranatha Ministries

*"**The Kingdom** is a timely END TIME message for all Believers to get ready for His return and open the heart of the unbelievers to accept Jesus Christ as their Lord and Saviour in their lives. MARANATHA"* Pastor Remegio C. Blanco – Philippines

*"Wow!! If you are confused about end times prophesy and what is on the horizon prophetically speaking, this new book: **The Kingdom** is for you!! It will challenge you, inspire you, and exhort you while it is still called day (John 9:4)!! The Spirit and the Bride say, 'Come, Lord Jesus'!!*
Theresa Ruth – Orlando, FL

Reader's Comments

"I cannot imagine how many Christians think that everything is "ok" just the way they are, not considering some of the most eternally necessary, but all too often neglected truths in God's Word. I truly hope that many people will read it and be blessed by its wealth of insightful and most <u>urgently</u> <u>needed</u> instruction regarding entering His glorious Kingdom."

James H. Adams – Lauderhill, FL

"What an insightful writing! The shepherds of the church today are missing some of the most important concepts the Bible teaches. The Armenian movement teaches one side of the picture, the Calvinist movement teaches another. Both have some truth, and both contain error. They fail to see the difference between the spirit and the soul of the Believer. Without this insight, they cannot see the complete picture. This book will help the Believer see the whole picture. Without that picture, the soul is in a great deal of danger. If you have been sitting under the teachings of either of these movements, please do not close this book prematurely. Read it from cover to cover, then read it again. The extent of gratitude we owe this man is beyond measure!" Karen Bishop – Glasgow, KY

*"I had the opportunity to meet Jim when he came to speak at a gathering called Maranatha Fellowship in Lakeland, Florida. It was through reading Jim's first book in 1998, **The Coming Spiritual Earthquake**, that it answered many questions that I had asked my pastor about in Matthew 25:1-13 about the ten virgins and the rapture. Jim's latest book on the Kingdom will help me to share and validate with others what I have been sharing with men and women for years about Outer Darkness and Gehenna, especially. I truly believe Jim Harman has a special anointing from El Elyon (the Most High) and a calling that will bless all of us who read his new book: **The Kingdom.**"*

Robin Wade – Ft. Pierce, FL

HELP DISTRIBUTE THIS MESSAGE

ARE YOU A WATCHMAN?
(Ezekiel 33:1-9)

Many Christians may not *"enter into"* the coming Kingdom if they don't hear the message in this timely book. Help get this *"strong meat"* to your friends and loved ones while there is still time!

Prophecy Countdown Publications does not have the resources to distribute this important message to all the bookstores. Since we believe this information is so vital for the Endtime Church, this PDF book is being made available for free at: www.ProphecyCountdown.com. Feel free to copy to your computer and e-mail to all those who you care about.

Order Books at Cost of Printing & Shipping*

# of Copies	Printing	Packaging	Postage	Author Profit	Total Cost	Cost / Book
1	$2.30	$0.80	$1.90	$0.00	$5.00	$5.00
3	$6.93	$0.90	$4.95	$0.00	$12.78	$4.26
5	$11.55	$1.00	$4.95	$0.00	$17.50	$3.50
10	$23.10	$1.25	$10.35	$0.00	$34.70	$3.47
16	$36.96	$1.55	$10.35	$0.00	$48.86	$3.05
36	$83.16	$2.55	$13.77	$0.00	$99.48	$2.76

*Order extra copies to give to friends and loved ones.

Order online at: www.ProphecyCountdown.com or send check to: Jim Harman
P.O. Box 941612
Maitland, FL 32794

The Day of the Lord is Near!

The Coming Spiritual Earthquake

by James T. Harman

"The Message presented in this book is greatly needed to awaken believers to the false ideas many have when it comes to the Rapture. I might have titled it: THE RAPTURE EARTH-QUAKE!"
Ray Brubaker - God's News Behind the News

"If I am wrong, anyone who follows the directions given in this book will be better off spiritually. If I am right, they will be among the few to escape the great-est spiritual calamity of the ages."
Jim Harman - Author

MUST READING FOR EVERY CHRISTIAN!
HURRY! BEFORE IT IS TOO LATE!